D0547212

The Art of
Divination

Practices from around the World

Konecky & Konecky
72 Ayers Point Rd.
Old Saybrook, CT 06475

ISBN: 1-56852-511-7

Printed and bound in China

Didier Blau

The Art of
Divination

Practices from
around the World

Illustrations by Linh Thai Duy

KONECKY&KONECKY

Foreword

S ince the dawn of time, men and women all over the world have tried to fathom the mystery of the future. "Messengers" such as shamans, magicians, priests, druids or soothsayers weave a link between the gods and human beings, as well as between the forces of the universe and their influences on our lives, our actions, and consequently our destinies.

Each of the methods of divination presented in this book has been adapted to the modern world so that you can easily make use of it in your everyday life and find answers to the questions that you are asking yourself today.

Each of these methods has its own manner of thinking, its own traditions and symbols, and its particular way of proceeding. Each one will appeal to you in its own way and answer certain questions. With time and practice, you will discover which ones suit you best and are most effective at responding to your concerns. You will develop your sensitivity, your imagination, and your ability to recognize and respect your feelings.

Approach the oracles with delicacy and good will. Finally, you must be aware that to preserve their value, the arts of divination must not be "practiced" too often. The maximum should be one question per person per day.

Now you can start practicing! For others and for yourself, become the "messenger" who combines wisdom and intuition, linking heaven and earth.

Divination around the world

The Ogham

Numerology

Darb er-Raml

Tonalamalt

Jogo dos buzios

7

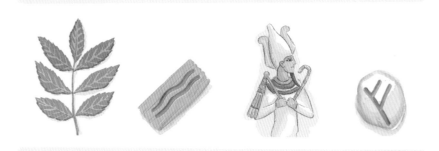

The **Ogham** of the Celts involves choosing a tree, whose symbol gives you guidance about your situation as it presents itself.

Venda tablets representing the members of a family are particularly good at responding to romantic questions.

The **oracle of ancient Egypt** expresses your strengths and weaknesses as well as revealing the outcome of your situation.

Mo, a Tibetan tradition, conjures up a poetic image that answers your questions.

Darb er-Raml, the oracle of the sand, involves drawing a symbol that reveals whether the omen for the future is favorable.

The **Tarot** (sometimes known as the Tarot of Marseilles) and its arcana describe the mental state of the person asking the question, the situation as it is, and how it will develop.

The choice of a symbol in the **Tonalamalt** or **Aztec Book of Destiny** will establish the prediction for the future according to the area and the question asked.

Colors and their associations deal with romantic relationships, your mental state, that of your partner, and what unites you or what separates you today.

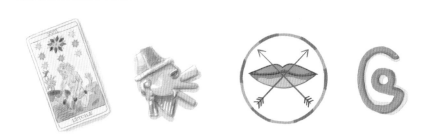

In **Zulu divination**, numbers and symbols give recommendations on your situation and its developments.

In the **Nordic runes**, the letters of the ancient Saxon alphabet, each letter emanates a special force and a prediction for the future of your romantic relationships.

The **I Ching**, an age-old Chinese oracle, clarifies your situation and suggests the best way of behaving.

Numerology is based on the symbolism of the numbers of your date of birth, which determine the trends of the next nine years.

The **Jogo dos buzios** is the mouthpiece of the Orixas. These Brazilian gods reveal whether you are benefiting from special favorable protection for your projects.

Mahabo, the Burmese art of divination, looks at the day of the week on which you were born and the time and day on which you are asking the question. It tells you whether the time is favorable for action.

Kumalak, the Kazakhstan art of divination, studies the mental state of the questioner as well as the questioner's feelings, situation, and destination.

The
Ogham

The Celtic
art of divination

Originally from Central Europe,
the Celts invaded the western
regions of Europe in the fifth
century bc. At that time the
Celtic world stretched from
Gaul as far as Scotland, including
Ireland, Wales, and Spanish Gali-
cia. The Celts read the future in
dreams, the shape of clouds, the
flight of birds, the skeletons of
animals, and in the Ogham, the
"secret language of the poets."
The Celts believed that trees
were the receptacles of cosmic
forces. By associating them with
the twenty letters of their alphabet, the druid or *frithir* interpreted the sacred signs: the
omens.

Consulting the oracle

The Ogham requires twenty wooden sticks about three inches long and a little under half an inch thick. If you can, make them yourself, since then they will be more charged with your own energy. Mark each one of them with the Celtic name of a tree, and then put them in a bag. When you have asked your question, take one stick out of the bag. You may also proceed without asking a particular question, in which case the oracle can be interpreted in a general sense.

Alternatively, use the wheel on the opposite page as follows:

1

Put your finger on a tree at random.

2

Choose a number between 10 and 30 and count this number of squares, clockwise or counterclockwise as you wish.

3

The tree you finish on is the oracle. Look up the associated symbol in the following pages and read the guidance it gives.

Interpretations

1 ● Beithe
BIRCH

Famous for its beauty in spring, the birch tree symbolizes a beginning. It involves energy, vitality, and rising force. It may indicate the start of a project, the beginning of a union, or the birth of a child. The birch acts as a protection because it brings luck, good fortune, and the promise of improvement. What is good will happen, and what is bad will go away.

Guidance
An important change is about to happen, but you must not be afraid of it. Rid yourself of what no longer meets your needs and have faith in the future. Do not lag behind this movement, but precede it. Good news is coming your way.

2 ● Luis
ROWAN

In Celtic tradition, the fruits of the rowan tree are the "food of gods," and the tree has magical properties. It acts as a protection against enchantment and evil spells. This symbol calls on your intuition. You must be perceptive and perfect your knowledge of the situation in which you find yourself. Then act, and you will achieve the success you hope for.

Guidance
The rowan evokes the hidden forces that are within you. Be careful not to be overcome by the impressions and intuitions that you are experiencing. Do not doubt yourself, or others will doubt you too.

3 • Fern
ALDER

4 • Sail
WILLOW

The special characteristics of the alder tree are that it does not rot in water, and that when you cut it the wood turns red. It is the symbol of strength and perseverance. The situation in which you find yourself needs tenacity and determination. You must remain firm and loyal to your principles and follow a more traditional path rather than an original one. Even if there is competition, you will end up the winner, but only if you remain true to yourself.

Guidance
You must be certain of your roots and your foundations, or everything will collapse in the medium term. You need to know when to change and when to preserve the status quo. Do not be afraid of defeat or failure. Remain honest and genuine. Act with clarity.

In Celtic tradition, the willow tree was used by witches as a medicinal plant that they boiled in their magic cauldrons. The willow grows near water, symbol of the unconscious. It therefore involves imagination, an intuition of the strengths that you have within you but of which you are not yet aware. It is within yourself or within your family circle or among your close friends that you will find the answers to your questions.

Guidance
You have a whole world inside you waiting to be discovered, and you must move in that direction. Be perceptive and shrewd, or even cunning if necessary. Then, in your present situation, you will be able to deal more easily with the unexpected dangers that could arise on your path.

5 ● Nnoin
ASH

6 ● Huath
HAWTHORN

The ash tree represents the link between your inner world and the external world. But it warns you to be careful. Indeed, you have a tendency to believe that things are as you see them. In your situation appearances are deceptive. You must exercise clear judgment, looking at the situation as a whole and not only at the details. You must understand how your actions lead to reactions. There is a close relationship between the two.

Guidance
Don't act yet. For the moment you must cut yourself off from the world, withdrawing a little and distancing yourself from things. You will then have a wider view of the situation, which will be a guarantee of your success.

The hawthorn with its sharp thorns that tear clothes does not have a good reputation in Celtic tradition, and its omen is not favorable. You have let yourself go, or you have committed excesses; now you are moving from "too much" to "too little," and this may refer to material matters or to emotional ones. The hawthorn also indicates a lack of self-esteem or the unconscious sabotage of your projects.

Guidance
You must rid yourself of what is weakening you or break your bad habits. Isolation and solitude are essential before you can start again. Do not act yet; remain patient and keep your problems to yourself. If you can reappraise your situation, you will achieve success. Otherwise, bad luck will pursue you.

7 • Duir
OAK

8 • Tinne
HOLLY

Symbol of power and stability, the oak is the tree of the druids, the great vessel receiving and storing cosmic forces, the sign of a heroic destiny, generous actions, and a noble heart. The situation in which you find yourself requires strength of character and endurance. Great joy awaits you, if you behave openly, naturally, and honestly.

Guidance
Now is a time for synthesis, to gather under your mantle all the people and forces that were scattered until now. If need be, don't hesitate to take control of operations, assuming the role of leader.

Always on the defensive, holly pricks anyone who gets too close. If your situation is not happy, you are feeling the effects of your bad actions in the past. You are now forced to unite opposing forces in order to find the proper balance.

Guidance
Like holly, which remains green through the winter, you must remain firm in adversity. There are problems to be overcome, and that will give you real strength. But for the moment, do nothing. You need to know more; you are not well enough informed, and you lack precise directions and objectives. In particular, if it is a problem of legal action or money, you should remain on the defensive.

9 • Coll
HAZEL

The hazel tree is an excellent omen because it represents creativity. It symbolizes a source of beauty and purity. It relates to communication, language, ideas, and knowledge. The situation in which you find yourself enables you to teach something to other people, but also to learn something from them. You have good judgment, you are in control of the situation, and you can act as referee and conciliator.

Guidance
You are capable of giving much to those around you. Talk, listen, communicate your knowledge, express your ideas, and follow your intuitions. Otherwise your creativity will dry up, and your talents will crumble away and become scattered.

10 • Queirt
APPLE

With its delicious, juicy fruit, the apple tree is the symbol of eternal youth. It expresses beauty, perfection, and love. The situation in which you find yourself is much to your advantage. Your task now is to harmonize what must be, to balance the forces around you, and to look for beauty and perfection in everything you do, in all aspects of everyday life.

Guidance
The apple tree invites you to live intensely, to live life to the full. Don't take on too much, don't try to do everything at the same time, but follow a single path, weighing up your efforts and letting your heart speak out. Yes, your best assets are to be found at the bottom of your heart.

11 •Muin
VINE

12 •Gort
IVY

The vine symbolizes wine. It is not a matter of losing consciousness but of becoming aware. The vine removes inhibitions, freeing you from logical and rational thought processes. It brings peace of mind, thus allowing you to find the solutions to your problems within yourself. It is a sign of good omen as long as you opt for simple ideas, living soberly without trying to impress or imitate others.

It hooks on, it clings, and it climbs… Ivy is the symbol of inner strength and tenacity. The situation in which you find yourself is developing. You are in the process of changing your habits, your lifestyle or your medium-term objectives. But this will take time. It will require patience and, in particular, courage, combined with great determination. In this way the transformations you are looking for will become reality.

Guidance
You are enthusiastic, but be sure to keep your feet on the ground. Don't let yourself be carried away by projects and desires. Do not go to the other extreme; in other words, do not become lazy or too self-indulgent. For the time being, patience is strongly recommended. Be objective and remain alert. You will probably meet someone who will help you.

Guidance
Throw yourself fully into what you are doing. Concentrate on the goal you are aiming at and the means of achieving it. Know what you want, draw up a plan in advance and stick to it. Like the ivy, cling to what you want.

13 • Ngetal
REED

14 • Straif
BLACKTHORN

The reed that grows near lakes and the sea symbolizes harmony. It is a sign of growth, good health, and well-being. The time has come to unify the various points of view, to regroup what is scattered, and to find the point of equilibrium. It is in this relational context, with your family, your partner or your close circle that you can now modify what already exists and improve your relationships. You can influence events and people. This is a good omen.

Guidance
You must guard against anxiety and unbridled imagination. You may be absent-minded and stray from the right path, to the point of not knowing what you want any more. Collect your thoughts, call upon other people, and look for common goals.

In Celtic tradition the blackthorn has a bad reputation, being the shrub of evil spells. It symbolizes forces that are stronger than you, problems, and physical or psychological constraints. In the current situation you do not control events or people. You do not even control yourself… You must move from the negative to the positive, from a restricted way of life to a new-found freedom.

Guidance
You are ruled by outside forces and unable to act freely. You need to become aware of this. You must exorcise your anxieties, put your problems into perspective, and show compassion towards yourself. Learn to recognize what you fear. Then everything will be easier.

15 • Ruis
ELDER

16 • Ailm
FIR

In Celtic tradition, the elder tree is associated with the color red, the color of its fruits, which are used to produce a dye. Red is the color of progress and action. For you, it is the transition from one state to another, a natural change that is beginning to take place. From a psychological point of view, it represents the passage from lack of concern to maturity. On a more practical level, it could herald a move or a journey.

Guidance
What is old will go away, while what is new will arrive. You must not only follow but also precede this evolution. Do not try to slow down this movement; do not cling to what is disappearing. Otherwise you might stagnate. The elder is telling you that the times are changing.

The fir tree is seen as an excellent omen. In Celtic tradition a branch is placed under the bed of a newborn baby. The fir represents good health, energy, and strength because it remains green all the year round. The situation in which you find yourself demands mental strength and objectivity, but above all it requires clarity. Now you can rise to a level where you will gain a clear view of the problem to be resolved.

Guidance
Weakness turns into strength, and your situation improves. But be careful, you must exercise a degree of control over others. Are you really capable of doing so? Is this really what you want? The danger contained in this message lies in exercising power without objectivity.

17 Onn
GORSE

18 Ur
HEATHER

With this symbol it is a matter of collecting together elements or people in order to turn them into something better. In your situation you must create a synthesis. You must bring together people, materials, ideas, and information. Call upon trustworthy people, try to understand and harmonize your relationships, and, in particular, do not act selfishly, for your own benefit only.

Guidance
It is not the time to take on too much. You have excellent trump cards that might lead to a radical change in your way of looking at life. But you must think of the common good, moving towards what is good and beautiful and distancing yourself from what is ugly, sad, and unhealthy.

Growing on moors, heather is the symbol of imagination and intuition, as well as of dreams, romance, and great outpourings of the soul. The unconscious takes precedence over consciousness, while what you feel deep down within you must come out and be expressed. It is a powerful feeling, more powerful than you are—it is a passion! You do not have a choice: you must do what you love to do. Opportunities will soon come your way and will drive you in that direction.

Guidance
Here the danger would be losing yourself in minor problems instead of doing what you love to do. You must act on your passions and not allow your passions to act on you. You need to express your inner self.

19   Edad
ASPEN

With its leaves rustling in the wind, the aspen tree represents an obstacle to be overcome. You are having difficulties or problems in your everyday life, but you must be determined to fight evil. This includes the evils that are outside you, but above all those that are within you: bad habits, narrow-mindedness, the fear of not matching up to what is expected of you, the fear of failure, and so on. This symbol says that you have the ability to overcome negative situations.

Guidance

Obstacles and resistance are becoming apparent, but you can overcome them. The aspen acts as a protection, an encouragement. But be careful not to help those who are opposing you…

20   Idad
YEW

The beautiful evergreen tree that is the yew has poisonous fruits. It is the tree associated with cemeteries, and its symbols are those associated with death and transformation. The yew represents the earth, roots, our forebears, those things that link us to our ancestors and what they have passed on to us. Here, death does not signify the end of life but the passage from one state to another, a narrow, difficult journey.

Guidance

The current situation involves a lack of comfort, a loss, frustration or a feeling of sadness. You must be fully aware of the transformations that are taking place in your life. Only then will you be able to move forward.

Venda tablets

In Africa the art of divination is based on symbols linked to natural forces, those that rule the elements, animals, and human beings. The Venda people of Zimbabwe use animal bones, wooden tablets, or flat stones to forecast the future. The forces of nature that the soothsayer calls upon—Rain, Fire, Wind, and Earth—are reflected in the ties that link the members of a family: the Mother, the Father, the Son, and the Daughter, each one the bearer of a message.

Consulting the oracle

1

Get four pieces of wood, flat stones or pebbles (or cut out four pieces of cardboard, each about two inches square). On one side only, draw the following symbols:

The Son

The Father

The Mother

The Daughter

The Father   Water, rain, seed, the life force.

The Mother   Fertile earth, the home, protection.

The Son   Fire, lightning, instinct, passion.

The Daughter   Air, wind, dispersal, charm.

2

If possible, go and sit outside on the ground. Put your question or ask the questioner to say it, out loud or silently.

3

Take the four symbols in your hands.
Squat down and concentrate for a few seconds. If you are using wooden tablets or flat stones, throw them on the ground. If using pieces of cardboard, throw them up in the air.

4

Study the result. The symbols that are hidden (face down) are "asleep" and these are removed. Look at the text that relates to the combination of symbols (or the single symbol) that are "open" or face up.

Example

"Open" symbols: Rain and Wind.
This combination: "The Father and the Daughter."

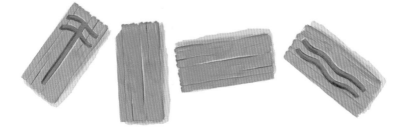

Interpretations

The Father

THIS TABLET STANDS FOR THE RAIN WATER THAT FERTILIZES THE EARTH, GIVING THE POWER OF LIFE, OF CREATION, STRENGTH, POWER, AND RICHES. IT REPRESENTS A MATURE, PROTECTIVE, WISE MAN..

Omen
Excellent in all areas. The time has come to take on responsibilities, to act with courage and firmness, and to know precisely what you want. If you do these things, you will certainly succeed!

If your question is about love
You control the situation and it is up to you to act. Therefore express your passion, take the initiative, show the way, and say what you want. Your partner will understand you and follow you.
- If you are a man, you have to make the first move.
- If you are a woman, the oracle predicts that you will meet a mature man or one older than you.

The Mother

THIS TABLET STANDS FOR THE NOURISHING, FERTILE EARTH, FAMILY LIFE, AND THE HOME. IT REPRESENTS A MATURE WOMAN OR A WOMAN WHO IS EXPECTING A CHILD..

Omen
For the time being do not undertake anything or start anything new. Listen to the world around you, attend to details, and protect those around you. People need you, your advice, and your time. Now is not the time to act but to welcome, to nourish, and to create.

If your question is about love
It is not up to you but to the other person to choose a direction or take a decision. You must follow rather than take the lead. For the moment, be patient, receptive, and malleable. Soon your hopes will be fulfilled.
- If you are a man, the oracle predicts that you will soon meet a mature woman or one who is older than you.
- If you are a woman, you can expect family happiness or the prospect of a birth.

The Son

THIS TABLET STANDS FOR FIRE, ENTHUSIASM, WARMTH, AND ENERGY. IT REPRESENTS A YOUNG MAN.

Omen

Fire animates you. You are like an adolescent, excited and impatient. You need to develop, change and become independent. In this situation, you must accelerate the pace. Take a few risks and be willing to shake things up.

If your question is about love

You are enlivened by the fire of your emotions. Now take the situation in hand and make the first move. Kick start a relationship by putting your cards on the table. This is the sign of an intensely romantic but unbridled relationship.

- If you are a man, be careful not to lose your head.
- If you are a woman, this tablet predicts the arrival of a young bachelor: a new partner is approaching…

The Daughter

THIS TABLET STANDS FOR AIR, WIND, MOVEMENT, AND DISPERSAL, BUT ALSO FOR CHARM. IT REPRESENTS A YOUNG GIRL, A YOUNG WOMAN, OR A CHILD.

Omen

This represents grace, beauty, and ease, attraction and pleasure. Your role is to bring harmony into the world around you and to create connections. Your freshness, innocence, and joie de vivre will make the situation develop.

If your question is about love

Journeys and opportunities for new encounters and friendships are coming your way—unless your feelings are too scattered, or your faithfulness is put to the test.

- If you are a woman, you have numerous trump cards; your charm is undeniable.
- If you are a man, there will soon be an encounter…

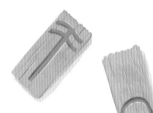

The Father and the Mother

WATER AND EARTH, THE TWO PRIMORDIAL FORCES, UNITE AND BECOME FERTILIZED. THEY PRODUCE ENERGY AND OFFER THEIR EXPERIENCE OF LIFE.

Omen
You are going to give or receive sensible advice and make an important decision. It will lead to the successful conclusion of your projects and the realization of your wishes. You projects will develop and flourish.

If your question is about love
Father and Mother, the fundamental couple, predict an encounter, a union, or a new equilibrium. There will be an improvement in your relationships, family harmony, sensual satisfaction, and sexual development, or even the birth of child!

The Father and the Son

WATER AND FIRE, THE TWO MALE ENERGIES, ARE HERE COMBINED, GENERATING STEAM AND MOTIVATION. THEY DRIVE YOU TO DO A LOT, PERHAPS EVEN TOO MUCH!

Omen
A force is sweeping you along irresistibly. An interesting project, a task that is hard to complete successfully or a competition is looming. There is a risk of going too far or causing tension. You must control the situation, ensuring that each person remains in their place and does not encroach on the other's territory.

If your question is about love
Is it a struggle for power, a challenge between suitors, or a matter of jealousy or infidelity? Whatever it may be, your emotional situation is about to change. Everything will go well as long as the partners feel free in their thoughts and actions, and they can maintain their independence.

The Father and the Daughter

WATER AND AIR COMBINE THE POWERFUL ENERGY OF THE FATHER AND THE LIGHTNESS OF THE TEENAGE GIRL.

Omen

Excellent news! Something original and unexpected is coming your way. A new life, new ideas, new contacts and encounters… This response is beneficial in all areas.

If your question is about love

The wind is blowing, while the moisture in the sky is regenerating the atmosphere and your state of mind. The way in which you see things and people is beginning to change. If your present situation does not suit you, you can be sure that things won't stay the same for long! Do not remain fixated on one thought or on one person. You will soon change your surroundings, your pace, your habits, or even… your partner!

The Mother and the Son

IN THIS COMBINATION, THE FIRE AND ITS ENERGY MUST NOT BURN THE EARTH AND EXHAUST IT, AND THE EARTH MUST NOT SUFFOCATE THE FIRE OF ACTION.

Omen

Energies are present, but they are difficult to channel. This is the sign of expansion, requiring that you control the situation by assessing your project before acting, and carefully balancing periods of action and periods of rest. Be careful, impatience could get you into trouble.

If your question is about love

There is every chance that you will succeed if you do not go over the top through your impulsiveness. But all the same, don't curb your enthusiasm! You must find the right balance between passion and wisdom, and between intellectual and sensual interests. There will also be the opportunity of an encounter during a journey or a move.

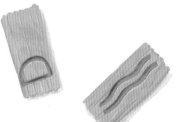

The Mother and the Daughter

EARTH AND AIR HAVE JOINED TOGETHER TO PRODUCE A LIGHT, SLIGHTLY FRIVOLOUS ATMOSPHERE; INDEED, THERE IS A LACK OF ENERGY AND MOTIVATION.

Omen

If there are no problems, there is no need for action. Don't ask yourself too many questions, take good care of yourself, and have a great time where you can. But watch your tongue to make sure you do not give away your secrets!

If your question is about love

Things that are interesting from a sentimental and sensual point of view are about to happen: an encounter, an exchange or a liaison, and perhaps also envy, jealousy, or gossip. Do not let yourself be influenced by what others say, do not try to look like somebody else. Remain yourself. Then you will be appreciated.

The Son and the Daughter

SINCE AIR FANS FIRE, THIS COMBINATION DEMONSTRATES THE SPONTANEITY AND ENTHUSIASM OF YOUTH BUT ALSO ITS IMPATIENCE, IMPETUOUSNESS, AND LACK OF EXPERIENCE.

Omen

You have enthusiasm, energy, and motivation. You will successfully complete your project as long as you curb your enthusiasm, think before you act, and see things in the longer term. In the present situation nothing is impossible, and there is no major problem. Time will work in your favor.

If your question is about love

You seem very excited and exhilarated by something or someone, or by a love affair that is just starting. Above all do not spread your feelings too thinly. For the moment, this relationship appears to lack maturity, but with time the situation will improve, and what you hope for will come true.

The Father, the Mother and the Son

DISHARMONY! FIRE BURNS THE EARTH AND WATER OVERFLOWS TO EXTINGUISH THE INFERNO...

Omen

This combination represents the rethinking of a situation, a dream, an illusion or an unconscious fear. Be careful! Someone or something seems to be rated too highly or, on the contrary, neglected. You must reassess the situation more carefully before you act or start work on the project that you are planning.

If your question is about love

Tensions, arguments, frustration or a lack of clarity in the liaison... your relationship appears unbalanced, there are questions worrying you, or loneliness weighs heavily upon you. For the time being, do not ask from the other person what you yourself are not capable of giving, but build on what already exists.

The Father, the Mother and the Daughter

THE PRESENCE OF AIR, THE DAUGHTER, IN THIS COMBINATION CREATES INSTABILITY, UNREST OR ARGUMENTS.

Omen

This represents a relationship problem, a confrontation, a role reversal that diminishes legitimate power and hierarchic authority or upsets the natural order of things. Before you can act it is important that each person regain his or her place, equilibrium, or role.

If your question is about love

The situation is complicated; your feelings are confused, or the other person's are vague. There is a lack of comprehension, an argument, an incident, a grain of sand that grates or, where applicable, the temporary halt or definitive end to a relationship. Be clearsighted about the other person and yourself. For the time being do not take any decision; do not go any further than the situation requires.

The Father, the Son and the Daughter

FANNED BY THE WIND, FIRE MAKES THE WATER BOIL, WHICH WARMS AND PURIFIES THE AIR.

Omen
This is a very good draw, particularly from an intellectual, relational, and spiritual point of view, rather than a purely materialist one. Do not try and be like someone else; be true to yourself and follow your own intuition. This will guide you more reliably than anyone else will, and your projects will succeed.

If your question is about love
You can, indeed you must, have confidence in yourself, your feelings, and the strength of your love. Ideas, projects, friendships, and encounters will flourish. Yes, you will be appreciated, people will follow you… and people will love you.

The Mother, the Son and the Daughter

EARTH, AIR AND FIRE… HERE IS A DRY, BRITTLE COMBINATION

Omen
Weakness, lack of honesty, disillusion, or deception? Something or someone is escaping you, and for the moment you are not in control of events. Remain clear-sighted and very careful in your relationships.

If your question is about love
You have been abandoned, disappointed or offended and your thoughts are gloomy. You are missing something or someone. Before you can succeed you must examine your conscience. You must appreciate and love yourself more. It is only on this condition that others will love you. Before anything else, regain your authority over yourself and exert self-control.

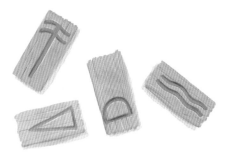 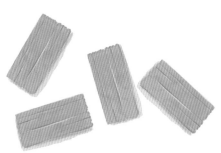

The Father, the Mother, the Son and the Daughter

ALL FOUR ELEMENTS ARE GATHERED HERE. THIS REPRESENTS PERFECT HARMONY WITH EACH ELEMENT ADDING TO THE OTHERS. IT IS THE UNION OF LOVE AND KNOWLEDGE, OF STRENGTH AND WISDOM.

Omen

The answer to your question is "yes," everything is fine and will become even better. You have drawn the best possible combination of Venda tablets!

If your question is about love

Your feelings are about to grow and blossom, and the omen for a union is favorable. If you are part of a couple, a new phase is about to begin. Your bonds are becoming stronger, and sexuality and sensuality are awakening. For the unattached, this response presages a future encounter…

All the symbols are hidden

THIS DRAW EXPRESSES A LACK OF ENERGY AND MOTIVATION, OR ENVY.

Omen

The answer to your question is "no." You are moving in the wrong direction. You must rest your body and mind in order to recover your strength. Assess the situation and review certain aspects of your projects. You will make another draw of the oracle later.

If your question is about love

Your thoughts are complex, obscure and secret. You are hiding something from someone or more probably from yourself. Unless your question is no longer relevant…

The oracle of
Ancient Egypt

All-powerful in a civilization where the divine (incarnated in dozens of gods and goddesses), natural forces, and temporal power were all interconnected and arranged according to a universal order, the priests of Ancient Egypt were masters of the art of magic and divination.

Consulting the oracle

1

Carve or draw the names or symbols of the magic powers on twenty flat stones, pieces of wood or, if not available, squares of cardboard.

2

Sit on the ground with the stones or pieces of wood, or sit at a table with the cards.

3

Take the twenty stones, tablets or cards in your hand.

4

Ask the questioner to put the question either out loud or silently.
If you are asking a question yourself, say it out loud.
If there is no particular question, you can interpret the oracle in a general sense.

5

Put the stones or pieces of wood in a bag. If you are using cards, place them on the table.

6

Take three symbols at random.
The first expresses your strengths.
The second reveals your weaknesses.
The third indicates the solution to the situation.

If you prefer to use the wheel below:

Put your finger on one of the numbered squares at random, then count 9 squares in the direction of your choice, and finally write down the number of the symbol found. Repeat the operation a second time, then a third time in order to obtain the three symbols.

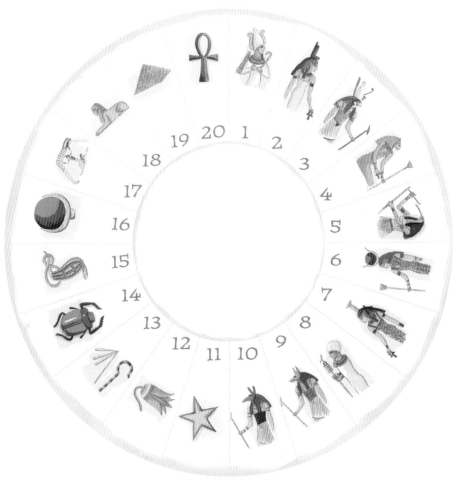

Interpretations

1 • Osiris
GOD OF FERTILITY AND GROWTH

First: Strengths
You have a balanced mind, spiritual strength, and a sense of responsibility and justice. In the image of Osiris, the father, you are a person others can rely on, and you have a certain authority.

Second: Weaknesses
Osiris is a very positive symbol and has no particular handicap or weaknesses.

Third: Solutions
This is a good omen since Osiris represents all that germinates, grows, and blossoms. Your projects will be successful if you proceed with gentleness and firmness and you trust your own judgment.

2 • Isis
SISTER AND WIFE OF OSIRIS, GODDESS AND MAGICIAN

First: Strengths
Your positive attributes are compassion, devotion, and gentleness. Like a mother caring for her children, you should look after those around you.

Second: Weaknesses
You do not feel really concerned by the situation, your help is not going in the right direction, you lack perseverance, or you are too possessive.

Third: Solutions
Love, sincerity and assistance to others. You must think more about others than about yourself. Isis promises satisfaction, especially if your question involves a birth, your children or your role as partner.

3 • Horus
THE SON OF OSIRIS AND ISIS,
THE EMBODIMENT OF POWER ON EARTH

4 • Bastet
GODDESS OF DANCE AND JOY,
PROTECTOR OF THE HOME.

First: Strengths
Your courage, your charisma, and your mental power are strengths you can count on. You are living up to your full potential.

First: Strengths
Bastet represents grace and beauty. Your strengths are your personality, your enjoyment of life, and your ability to follow your intuition.

Second: Weaknesses
Be wary of any desire for vengeance, eccentricity, passion or aggressiveness because this would lead to discord, a tense or complicated situation.

Second: Weaknesses
Guard against indifference, superficiality, anxiety, or sadness without reason. There is the risk of cutting yourself off from the world or of losing interest in it.

Third: Solutions
Good omen. There is a battle you will win, a recovery, a new family harmony, or the presence of a partner with undeniable charm!

Third: Solutions
You are protected, especially from a spiritual point of view. Current problems will disappear and pleasure will return… You will make the most of it.

5 • Thoth

GOD OF KNOWLEDGE, THE INVENTOR
OF WRITING, PATRON OF SCRIBES.

First: Strengths

Your intelligence and the way you express it through words are your main assets. It is through study, respect for the law, and reflection that you will achieve success.

Second: Weaknesses

You must guard against vanity and pride. Talk no more than is necessary, unless people have judged you wrongly, or you have judged others wrongly.

Third: Solutions

This response is a favorable one, particularly if your question is about studying or some other intellectual program. If you can be patient, fortune will smile upon you and the unexpected will play a beneficial role.

6 • Hathor

GODDESS OF LOVE
AND SENSUALITY

First: Strengths

Your charm and your ability to make the best of yourself are definite assets, but you are also well-grounded. You know what you want and what you don't want.

Second: Weaknesses

You are easily intimidated, you have an inferiority complex, and you are indecisive. These traits could put you in a bad position, unless they arise from your desire to live easily, in a relaxed manner, one day at a time.

Third: Solutions

An omen of blossoming and satisfaction, especially in love. There is pleasure in store for you that you can share with others. Hathor is the goddess of sensuality…

7 • Nephthys

WIFE OF SETH, SHE PARTICIPATES
IN THE RESURRECTION OF THE DEAD

8 • Ptah

ARCHITECT OF THE UNIVERSE,
PATRON OF CRAFTSMEN AND SCULPTORS

First: Strengths

Your strength lies in what cannot be seen. It is your sensitivity to people and situations, your reserve, your inner calm, and your silence that will guide you in the right direction.

First: Strengths

Ingenuity, creativity, and dexterity are your trump cards. This involves creating something tangible, visible, and material. You are on the way to constructing something.

Second: Weaknesses

You have hidden fears or anxieties that you are unable to express. Do not be taken in by illusions and false hopes, because in your situation you know less than you think!

Second: Weaknesses

Is it the refusal to accept responsibility, to contribute to the community, the fear of doing wrong, or of not being up to things? Whatever the case may be, your mind is not seeing things in a positive light.

Third: Solutions

A change cannot be made effectively. The situation is not clear, your intentions are vague, and the answers are still concealed. You must learn to see the situation more clearly.

Third: Solutions

Your situation will develop because your mind is open to progress. You are going to build a solid foundation and make progress, if you learn from the lessons of the past and remember them.

9 • Anubis
GUARDIAN OF TOMBS, PATRON OF EMBALMERS

First: Strengths
You are protected by mysterious forces that guide you in the right direction in spite of the pitfalls and ambushes—unless it is you who is acting as a guide to others.

Second: Weaknesses
You lack tact, diplomacy, and a sense of humor, or you have taken a wrong turn. Someone is playing tricks on you.

Third: Solutions
Movement, travel, and discoveries… Be prepared for action even if it appears difficult or uncertain. Anubis will guide and protect you.

10 • Seth
RULER OF THE DESERT AND OF DARKNESS

First: Strengths
You are facing opposition, difficulties or upsets. However it is not the others or outside conditions that are the cause of your problems, but yourself!

Second: Weaknesses
There may be a jealous, envious person with bad intentions towards you, whose influence is harmful to you. Or perhaps it is you who is jealous or envious.

Third: Solutions
The project you are working on cannot be carried out. You must question everything that no longer fits the present situation. You must destroy in order to rebuild on sounder, more solid foundations.

11 • Sirius

SACRED STAR WHOSE RISING ANNOUNCED
THE FLOODING OF THE NILE

First: Strengths

Sirius represents physical strength, endurance, a spirit of adventure, and the awareness of the importance of acting for the common good. You want to uplift yourself and shine, which is a good sign.

Second: Weaknesses

Torn between obstinacy and sloppiness, between aggressiveness and submission, you are still searching for the right direction. Watch out for physical and verbal violence, and don't let yourself be overcome by a persecution complex.

Third: Solutions

This is the sign of a sudden, unexpected change in the way you look at the situation. Take a longer view, stand back, and open your mind to innovation. If you do so you are sure to achieve success.

12 • The Lotus

IMAGE OF THE BIRTH OF THE SUN
EMERGING BETWEEN ITS PETALS

First: Strengths

The lotus, the sacred flower of Egypt, is an invitation to meditation and spiritual development. Your strength lies in the peaceful way in which you allow situations to unfold.

Second: Weaknesses

Like your mind, your body is experiencing restlessness, anxiety, and nervousness. You are withdrawing into yourself and preventing your deep inner self from expressing itself. Guard against introversion.

Third: Solutions

It is only by relaxing your inner tension and living a healthy lifestyle that you will achieve your aims. Learn not to worry, learn to feel safe, and be reassured that in the end everything will be all right.

13 ● The Crook and the Flail
EMBLEMS OF THE PHARAOH'S AUTHORITY

First: Strengths
With discipline, a sense of leadership, and natural authority, you have all you need to change your situation. But perhaps you are not aware of this?

Second: Weaknesses
You lack tolerance and forbearance, or you are using force to control or even dominate the situation, regulating the behavior of others. Don't try and do everything yourself.

Third: Solutions
A good omen for taking on responsibilities or for making important decisions. If you feel capable of it, accept a leading role; otherwise leave the command of operations to others.

14 ● Uraeus
SYMBOL OF PROTECTION, ASSOCIATED WITH THE SUN GOD

First: Strengths
You are perceptive, skilful, and wise, and this helps you to control events. Your strengths are considerable, and you should be aware of this.

Second: Weaknesses
Be careful. You are playing against forces stronger than you, you do not see the danger, you are pressed by time, or you are overcome by passion.

Third: Solutions
For you it is all or nothing! If your intentions are pure and devoid of selfishness, you will achieve great success. On the other hand, if you only act for yourself, you will fail.

15 • The Solar Disc
SYMBOL OF THE UPLIFTED SPIRIT

First: Strengths
Inspiration, wisdom, ideas to carry out… You are trying to grow, to raise yourself up, or to develop a new lifestyle more in line with your deeper aspirations. This is a good omen.

Second: Weaknesses
Be careful, you are accepting certain ideas as if they were true without having thought about them. Pause for a moment and look at the situation more objectively. Otherwise you will fail to see the truth, and in the end you will be disappointed.

Third: Solutions
The aim is not to stabilize but to transform. The omen is excellent for starting a project, traveling, and rising above difficulties. Your efforts will be crowned with success.

16 • The Twins
CHOU, GOD OF THE AIR, AND HIS SISTER AND WIFE TEFNOUT, GODDESS OF THE CLOUDS

First: Strengths
You have many talents, especially regarding associations, unions, and encounters. You work effectively as part of a team, enjoy family life, and adapt well to your environment.

Second: Weaknesses
You have difficulties in expressing your feelings, exchanging ideas, or being part of a group. Be careful not to be too selfish or too individualistic, otherwise you will remain an outsider.

Third: Solutions
An excellent omen for those who want to join with others and harmonize their relationships. You will achieve success, if you agree to become part of a group or a couple.

17 ● The Sphinx
LION WITH A HUMAN HEAD,
BENEVOLENT GUARDIAN.

18 ● The Scarab
SYMBOL OF THE SUN GOD AT SUNRISE
AND, BY ASSOCIATION, OF THE PHARAOHS

First: Strengths
Patience is your main asset. Know how to wait for the right time to act and keep what you feel to yourself … Silence is golden!

Second: Weaknesses
You have committed an indiscretion, you have displayed indifference towards others, a mystery must be solved, or perhaps something is happening behind your back.

Third: Solutions
It is no use discussing things or arguing about them. For the time being, remain discreet about your intentions, making sure you keep your secrets to yourself. Observe, but say nothing. Only time will provide an answer to your questions.

First: Strengths
This symbol bodes well, if you are trying to change a situation, to start again from scratch, or to set off again on the right foot. The scarab symbolizes a revival, a renaissance.

Second: Weaknesses
You have made a rather unwise change, you have been negligent, you have destroyed a situation, or you are feeling resentful. Now you are face to face with yourself.

Third: Solutions
Changes in your lifestyle, an upheaval, or a new departure may be in the offing. The prospects are good for those who are willing to live differently and to act in an unconventional way.

19 • The Pyramid
SYMBOL OF THE DEVELOPMENT
OF THE SOUL THROUGH TIME

20 • The Ankh
THE CROSS OR KEY OF LIFE, THE
EMBODIMENT OF THE BREATH OF LIFE

First: Strengths
Seeing things in the long term, keeping a firm hold of the situation… this is what you must do achieve your aim. The objective is not to transform things but to stabilize and even strengthen them.

First: Strengths
Living and loving… this is what this symbol represents. All you have to do is live for love, and love in order to live.

Second: Weaknesses
You have been negligent and happy-go-lucky, or you have tried to maintain the status quo against all odds. Get out of your rut, even it feels comfortable.

Second: Weaknesses
You have rejected or neglected someone, refused love or sought to find love without giving it. You have the key, but you cannot find the keyhole! Now you must pass through a narrow door.

Third: Solutions
A good omen provided that you stay the course and try to build solid, lasting bonds. Whatever the area concerned, everything that relates to long-term prospects is favorable.

Third: Solutions
A beautiful omen! It speaks of an encounter, blossoming sexuality, a warm relationship, a marriage, and a birth. Your friendships and romantic relationships will flourish.

Mo

During their meditations, Tibetan lamas recite six syllables, each one bearing a particular force or idea. **AH** represents space; **RA** represents power; **PA** is peace; **TSA** is destruction; **NA** is prosperity; **DHI** is the mind. Mo, one of the many Tibetan methods of divination, is based on the combinations of these syllables, which identify the image revealing the message.

Consulting the oracle

1
Find a die.

2
Ask the question or have someone else ask it.

3
Close your eyes and meditate for a little while. Let thoughts flow into your mind and let them flow out again as if they were just passing through.

4
Throw the die. Match the number thrown with its syllable as follows:

is AH   is RA   is PA

is TSA   is NA   is DHI

5
Throw the die again to obtain the second syllable.

6
Then read the image that corresponds to the combination of the two syllables. This is the answer to your question.

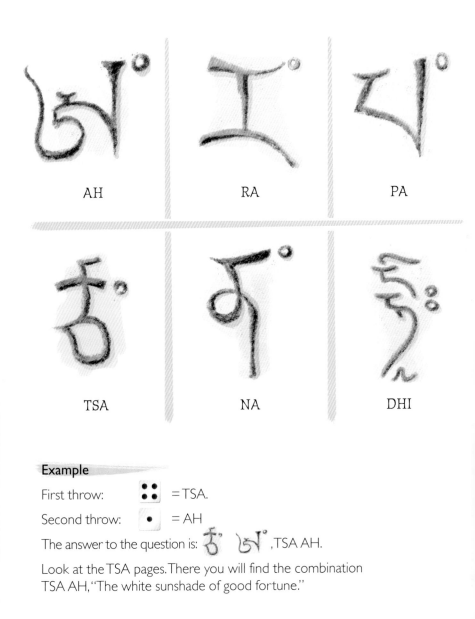

AH	RA	PA
TSA	NA	DHI

Example

First throw: ⚃ = TSA.

Second throw: ⚀ = AH

The answer to the question is: , TSA AH.

Look at the TSA pages. There you will find the combination TSA AH, "The white sunshade of good fortune."

Interpretations

AH AH
THE CLEAR SKY

Like a cloudless, clear blue sky, your heart must be absolutely pure and devoid of resentment, jealousy, or envy. Don't ask anything, don't play any role, just let things happen. Don't try to hold someone back or keep a situation from changing. In this way your projects will come to fruition. Indeed, the answer to your question is "yes." Your health, your family, and your traveling are protected, and you need not fear any obstruction.

AH PA
THE MILKY RAYS OF THE MOON

The moon is rising, and a milky light is filling the night. This omen deals particularly with love, sensations and feelings. You must act gently and peacefully in areas that require tact or artistic skills. There will be no struggle; no radical decision need be taken. Be tolerant and conciliatory especially towards yourself. Learn how to reassure and appreciate yourself… love yourself. In this way you will achieve well-being.

AH RA
THE FLAMING RAYS OF THE SUN

When the rays of the sun appear, they clear the fog and bring out the colors of life. The omen is good because the questions you are asking yourself will be answered, and confused situations will become clear. There is no need to be anxious, since your family, health, and friendships are protected. New paths are opening up, and your confidence is returning, as is your clear-headedness. You need fear no obstacle; rely on your own strengths, and you will succeed.

AH TSA
THE SPARKLING STAR

Like the star, which shines for a long time, you must not waste your strength or concern yourself with things that are not worth the trouble. This omen is positive and particularly favors journeys and moving. It is not a question of seeing a tangible result in the immediate future but of maintaining the right frame of mind. Remain open to opportunities. You will succeed in your enterprise as long as you are responsive, inquisitive and adaptable.

AH NA
THE GROUND COVERED WITH GOLD

The earth produces magnificent fruits, if
you cultivate it with care. You will succeed
in your enterprise as long as you do not
expect immediate results. Give priority
to patience and steadfastness. Look at
the development of the situation in the
long term. Travel or impulsive actions are
not involved. Continue on your way with
determination, and a little later you will
reap what you have sown.

AH DHI
THE SPARKLING DIAMOND

It is not in the outside world that you
will find the answers to your questions
but deep within your own mind, which
must peaceful and serene. You must be
in agreement with yourself, your words
must follow your thoughts and your
actions must follow your words. Then
everything will be all right. You will receive
good news, and you will achieve success.
This omen is particularly favorable to
students, artists, and writers.

RA AH

THE SHINING LAMP

The lamp radiates its light through the darkness and then makes it possible to distinguish good from evil. For the moment your mind is confused and in the dark, and you cannot find a solution to your problems. Don't expect any help or encouragement—only you can clear the mists so as to see the situation more clearly. This omen is favorable provided that you see people and things as they really are and not as you would like them to be…

RA PA

THE DEMON OF DESTRUCTION

This omen is clearly unfavorable. Your mind is not pure, your thoughts are not healthy, and you are moving in the wrong direction. Here you are not trying to build but to destroy. There is envy, jealousy, and resentment. If you do not change your frame of mind, you will not get anywhere. All you will achieve will be the destruction of relationships or the failure of your project. Don't let yourself be dragged downwards but aim high in an unbiased manner.

RA RA

FAT ON THE FIRE

This is a very favorable omen that expresses joy and contentment. You will soon reach the objective that you are pursuing, your desires will be satisfied, and you will shortly receive encouraging news. If you are sad, hide it, and if you are happy, show it. It is your enthusiasm, the desire to share your joy, and the need to make others happy that will lead to contentment.

RA TSA

THE ALL-POWERFUL KING

This is an oracle of good omen for flinging yourself into a fight, for acting forcefully and with determination, because your strength is increasing. It will be advantageous to make decisions, accept responsibilities, or seek to acquire authority. It will be unfavorable to hesitate, move backward, or avoid taking risks. The forces that are in you must be expressed, otherwise they will rapidly diminish.

RA NA
THE UNWATERED TREE

A tree that is not watered produces no fruit. This image indicates that your mind is not irrigated by good intentions. You are influenced by someone, or perhaps you are trying to imitate others. This means you are not following your own path. This is not good. As far as your question is concerned, the prospects are dim. Your wishes are confused, you are deluding yourself, and you are pursuing a dream. Can you ever reach it?

RA DHI
THE GATE TO FAVORABLE VISIONS

This is a beautiful omen! Your mind is turned towards that which is positive. It does not involve projects to be carried out or decisions to be taken. It is your imagination that will lead you on the road to success. All you need to do is to visualize your objectives, making them concrete in your mind, and they will become a reality in your life. You will helped by a kind person or a friend.

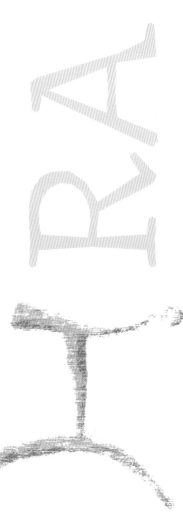

PA AH
THE JAR OF NECTAR

The omen is favorable so long as you make friends with peaceful, conscientious people whose relationship with you is not based on force. You will bring your project to a successful conclusion, although it may not be as satisfactory as you might have expected at the beginning. This oracle is especially favorable if your question is about finances or friendship.

PA PA
THE OCEAN OF NECTAR

The conditions are very favorable and, like the ocean, your possibilities are numerous, almost endless. Material and professional areas are favorably situated. It is the right time to ask for a raise or a promotion or to invest money in an enterprise. On the other hand, the omen for romance is less favorable, because you are acting only for your own benefit.

PA RA
THE DRIED-UP SPRING

This oracle speaks of pointlessness. Your objectives do not measure up to your powers, your mind is confused, and you are sad or disappointed, or you have a very blinkered view of the situation. The omen is rather discouraging, especially concerning romance or friendship. Change your way of looking at things, be generous and disinterested, and water will flow from the spring once more.

PA TSA
THE STORM

The wind is rising, and currents are raging! The omen is negative. Your mind is tormented. You no longer see things clearly, you are wrong about what others are thinking, or you are dealing with people with a bad influence on you who judge and condemn you. For the moment, do not act and do not make any decisions. Wait until you have recovered your peace of mind before carrying out your project.

PA NA
THE GOLDEN LOTUS

The lotus, the sacred flower of the Buddhists, is an excellent omen. Your good intentions are increasing, your situation is becoming clearer, you are regaining your strength, and the help you are given is more effective. Your wishes will be granted and, gradually, you will achieve success and well-being. If your present situation is not yet very good or very stable, be confident that everything will get better and better.

PA DHI
THE SOURCE OF HAPPINESS

The source of happiness exists… it is within you. It is not "somewhere else" or "later" that you will be happy, it is here and now. If you appreciate what you already have, if you do not try and cling to someone or to a situation, and if, in addition, you know that everything comes to an end, good things as well as bad, you will have found the source of happiness.

TSA AH
THE WHITE SUNSHADE OF GOOD FORTUNE

"Flowers always bloom at the right time." Your questions, your fears, and your anxieties are without real foundation. Don't worry about the current situation. Everything needs time to mature and develop, and it is no good trying to speed things up. There is neither a decision to be made nor any energetic action to be taken; take your time and live only in the moment.

TSA RA
THE SWORD OF FLAME

You have numerous talents, in particular great powers of persuasion. The omen is favorable, and your projects will be successful as long as you use these powers. Now is a good time for knocking on doors, declaring your love, expressing your desires, taking decisions, and arming yourself for a fight. You have the power to influence events, so use it.

TSA PA
PAPER IN THE WIND

"How to catch a piece of paper that is swept away by the wind? Who is capable of doing that?" For the moment, you are not. Indeed, your mind is exposed to all weathers, shaken by a thousand impressions, and influenced by evil people. You cannot reach the objective you have set yourself because it does not suit you. A separation is likely.

TSA TSA
THE GLORIOUS BANNER

The situation you are finding yourself in is good, and the time has come to express your potential. Action is a source of success. The omen is good for visiting, traveling, or moving. Look for social success, renown, or the announcement of happy news such as a marriage or a birth..

TSA NA
THE TREE STRUCK BY LIGHTNING

The omen you have drawn is not favorable. It involves obstruction, difficulties that cannot easily be surmounted. The situation is not to your advantage. There are tensions around you, and your partner does not understand you. Your mind is confused, and your heart is heavy. Do not continue with your project in this condition. Don't compound matters; examine your own mistakes before criticizing others.

TSA DHI
THE HOUSE OF
GOOD NEWS

You are reaching the top of the mountain, and you can see the house of good news. This is a very favorable omen, your wishes will be granted, your work will be done, and your romantic attachments will get stronger. Look no further than what is within your reach, and be prepared to welcome this good news.

NA AH

THE MOUNTAIN OF GOLD

The mountain of gold symbolizes stability. If your question is about a social position, it will be secure, if it is about a romantic relationship, it will be a faithful one, and if it is about financial gain, it will be considerable. Your decisions must be firm and your mind resolute. There is nothing you have to change; your mental stability will lead to success.

NA PA

THE JEWELED SHIP

This is a very favorable oracle, synonymous with prosperity. Your frame of mind is positive, and this promises well-being and satisfaction. Expect material riches, pleasure, and happy moments to share. The soil is fertile, and there is no enemy to be feared. For the moment, appreciate what you have, and do not try continually to increase your possessions. You will simply secure what is yours by right.

NA RA

THE DEMON OF DESIRE

Your mind is ruled by demons. You are driven by envy, a desire for power, sexual passion, or the need to accumulate material possessions. In Buddhist philosophy this can only lead to mistakes, mistakes for which you must now pay. As you only have your own interests at heart, you behave selfishly, you build barriers, and you are facing obstacles that you have created yourself.

NA TSA

THE MOUNTAIN OF SAND

You are like a mountain of sand, high perhaps but definitely unstable. All the more so now that the wind is blowing. The omen involves a reduction or a deterioration. Your relationships are crumbling, your position is weakening, your savings are dwindling, or you are putting yourself down. The oracle is rather negative. You have made bad choices or you are following a course that is not right for you. Reappraise your projects or, better still, reappraise yourself.

NA NA
THE RED CASTLE

Whether it be a romantic relationship or a social position, you are in the process of building something, and you are going in the right direction. The oracle is positive for acquiring money or influence and enriching love and friendship, but it is unfavorable for traveling, leaving a job or asking for help from your superiors. Perseverance and effort will help you achieve your objective.

NA DHI
THE TREASURE

Drawing the NA DHI oracle is like opening a treasure chest. It speaks of satisfaction and success. Your efforts will pay off, your projects are placed under favorable auspices, and you will obtain excellent results. Do not give in to impatience, do not focus on a single point but remain confident and calm. Then you will be able to open the treasure chest…

DHI AH

THE WAY OF BUDDHA

Following the way of Buddha is to understand that nothing is forever, that nothing can ever be taken for granted. It means not trying to cling to things out of fear of losing them. On the contrary you must let yourself go with the flow of life and live for the moment. Following the way of Buddha means never judging or criticizing other people or yourself. In this way you will achieve great success, and your wishes will be granted.

DHI RA

THE FLOWER GARDEN

This oracle speaks of beauty, pleasure, and love. It is particularly auspicious for relationships. Your intentions are good; you are looking for union and harmony. You have every chance of achieving your objective provided you do exactly what you want. Follow your intuition. Learn how to speak to yourself and listen to yourself. Then you will be able to enter the flower garden.

DHI PA

THE LUMINOUS FISH

This oracle speaks of mental and physical agility. Like the fish that moves easily in the ocean, your mind must be sharp, alert, and receptive to the signals sent out to you. Here the omen is positive in all fields as long as you do not upset anyone and remain flexible and diplomatic. Be careful not to lie to yourself.

DHI TSA

PLEASANT MUSIC

This oracle is a good omen. You will hear pleasant voices and sweet sounds of music. This voice may be that of your beloved who fulfils your expectations or that of a superior who talks to you with kindness. There is good news coming your way. The oracle is particularly positive about everything concerning study, writing, communication, foreign languages, and exchanges of ideas.

DHI NA
THE CHARIOT'S WHEEL

The wheel goes round, the chariot is advancing, and situations are developing. The omen is positive. You will achieve your aim but not immediately, because you have not yet reached the end of the journey. Some relationships still need to be harmonized; there is still work to be done and adjustments to be made. Do not focus on the present, but look at the development of the situation in the long term. Persevere and you will achieve success a little later on.

DHI DHI
THE VICTORIOUS STANDARD

Trumpets are resounding as you raise the standard of victory! The omen is very positive, but you must still fight or place yourself under the protection of someone in power. Then you will overcome every obstacle and win through. On a more personal level, you will gather around you all the people you love. You have all the assets to succeed, now it is up to you to move towards your objective.

Darb er-Raml

The oracle of the sand

Since time immemorial Arab soothsayers have practiced geomancy, the art of reading the signs of man's future in the sand of the desert. This method of divination is described in *The Thousand and One Nights*: "The magician wanted to find out the details of Aladdin's death. He pulled out the divining sand table from the back of a cupboard, sat on a square mat in the middle of a circle drawn in red, smoothed down the sand, arranged the male and female points, muttered geomantic formulae, and said: "Let us see, O sand, let us see! And how did he die, this scoundrel Aladdin?" As he said these words, he shook the sand according to the ritual. Then all of a sudden the pictures appeared…"

Consulting the oracle

1

If you have some sand or soil near you, take a wooden stick and use it to mark the boundary of the space in which you will question the oracle. Otherwise take a pencil and a piece of paper.

2

Ask for silence. Concentrate, then ask the question yourself or have someone else ask the question, out loud or silently.

3

Using the wooden stick, draw a row of small vertical strokes in the sand at random, without counting them. Alternatively use the pencil and draw the vertical strokes on the paper in the same way.

4

Repeat the operation another three times, arranging the rows below one other.

5

Write the number of strokes next to each row. If the number is even, draw a rod; if it is uneven, draw a dot.

Example

14 strokes:

6 strokes:

9 strokes:

8 strokes:

Answer to your question:
el-Bayâd,
"whiteness."

6

Read the interpretation corresponding to the picture made by the lines and dots obtained.

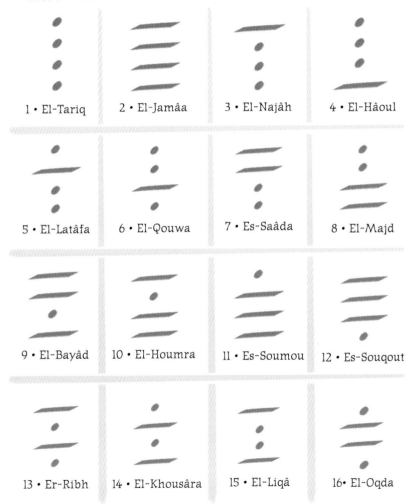

1 • El-Tariq   2 • El-Jamâa   3 • El-Najâh   4 • El-Hâoul

5 • El-Latâfa   6 • El-Qouwa   7 • Es-Saâda   8 • El-Majd

9 • El-Bayâd   10 • El-Houmra   11 • Es-Soumou   12 • Es-Souqout

13 • Er-Ribh   14 • El-Khousâra   15 • El-Liqâ   16• El-Oqda

Interpretations

1 • El-Tarîq
THE WAY

Symbol
El-Tariq is like fire suddenly bursting out. It is a way, a road, or a runway. Its nature is masculine, impulsive, spontaneous, direct, and undisciplined.

Meaning
This figure describes the road along which you are progressing. Soon things will change, and new situations will shake up your routines. There could be journeys, separation, detachment, liberation or newly found independence.

Attitude to adopt
Be ready to take a trip, to act on your own, or to cast off old habits.

If your question asks for a "yes" or "no" answer: This reading is favorable but does not provide a "yes" or "no" answer.

2 • El-Jamâa
THE GATHERING

Symbol
This figure represents rich, dense, fertile soil. It shows a gathering, a group or a crowd. It represents anonymity, dependence, passiveness, and receptivity.

Meaning
El-Jamâa announces instability and turmoil. You are surrounded by a thick fog and filled with a multitude of impressions and feelings. For the moment, there is not yet any clear path; everything is possible.

Attitude to adopt
In this confusion you must remain lucid, separate the true from the false and make up your own mind. Do not look for independence but join forces, cooperate, share.

If your question asks for a "yes" or "no" answer: This reading is favorable but does not provide a "yes" or "no" answer.

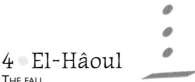

3 • El-Najâh
SUCCESS

Symbol
El-Najâh symbolizes spring water, pure and fresh. It promises ascent, uplift, benevolence, honesty, and legitimacy.

Meaning
This figure represents something that is starting, progressing and developing. It is a picture of good omen, indicating that a beneficial change is about to take place. Worries are now a thing of the past; everything is moving towards improvement and greater awareness.

Attitude to adopt
You should follow your intuition, open up to someone else or other people without fearing criticism and jealousy. Then your hopes will be rewarded with success.

If your question must be answered by a yes or no: This picture replies "yes," of course!

4 • El-Hâoul
THE FALL

Symbol
Here is a smoldering fire that slowly destroys. Expect a fall, separation, discord, immorality, selfishness, laxity, jealousy, secrecy, and lies.

Meaning
This figure means decline. Negative forces are bubbling up the surface. You are faced with illusion, danger, and conflict. It also represents the world of duplicity, false promises, and rumors.

Attitude to adopt
This destructive picture is not all bad. Indeed this destruction, this change in your frame of mind, will enable you to start again from scratch or to understand the reasons behind a failure.

If your question requires a "yes" or "no" answer: The answer is "no."

5 ● El-Latâfa
SWEETNESS

Symbol
This figure represents fresh air, light and soft. It expresses youth, elegance, affection, sensuality, art, and beauty in all its forms.

Meaning
El-Latâfa promises love, pleasure, cheerfulness, and a relaxed way of life. It foretells good times, especially in the field of creativity and romance.

Attitude to adopt
Learn to live in the present and enjoy the opportunities that life offers you, but guard against thoughtlessness and carelessness.

If your question requires a "yes" or "no" answer: This reading is favorable but does not provide a "yes" or "no" answer.

6 ● El-Qouwa
STRENGTH

Symbol
This figure represents explosive fire. It expresses combat, struggle, rebellion, instinct, virility, violence, anger, jealousy, and indulgence in sensual pleasure.

Meaning
El-Qouwa indicates enthusiasm and the need to dominate, which will lead to action. You will feel an increase in strength, but don't allow it to degenerate into aggressiveness and rebellion.

Attitude to adopt
You must have freedom at any cost. But be careful: you must guard against excess and go no further than the situation demands.

If your question requires a "yes" or "no" answer: The answer is "no."

7 • Es-Saâda
HAPPINESS

8 • El-Majd
GLORY

Symbol
Es-Saâda depicts fertile, cultivated soil. It expresses harmony, flowering, stability, success, honor, expansion, ambition, control, attraction, and fame.

Meaning
This figure denotes the fulfillment of wishes, satisfaction, reward for your efforts, the success of your enterprise, and deserved recognition.

Attitude to adopt
Seize all the opportunities that present themselves, favoring honesty and generosity. Good fortune will smile upon you, your projects will be successful, and you will experience happiness.

If your question requires a "yes" or "no" answer: This response is the best there is, and the answer is of course "yes!"

Symbol
El-Majd depicts a clear, lively fire but one that is short-lived if it is not constantly fanned. It expresses fragile happiness, transitory success, celebrity and the criticism it entails, and ruthless ambition... the ephemeral quality of fame.

Meaning
This figure refers to a passing opportunity that must be seized as it presents itself. It represents success, but an isolated success without any decisive impact on the direction of your life.

Attitude to adopt
Act, be bold and ambitious, but don't let success go to your head. This is just a stage. It may not last.

If your question requires a "yes" or "no" answer: This figure provides a qualified "yes."

9 • El-Bayâd
WHITENESS

Symbol
This figure represents fine, light earth. It expresses transparency, purity, innocence, serenity, chastity, spirituality, indulgence, and tolerance.

Meaning
The idea contained in this figure is clarity and contentment. It is about simple happiness, the search for truth, clear ideas, and healing.

Attitude to adopt
Be ready to listen, to help others, and to moderate your appetites. Avoid being impulsive or passionate. Try to resolve conflicts and find a kind of innocence in simplicity.

If your question requires a "yes" or "no" answer: This response should be probably be taken as "yes."

10 • El-Houmra
REDNESS

Symbol
This figure represents stagnant water. It warns of danger, passion, lack of discipline, upheaval, impulsiveness, temerity, vanity, excessive sensitivity, aggressiveness, and criticism.

Meaning
Sudden outbursts, conflicts, rebellion… the fire of passion is devouring you. What has been stagnant for too long must now progress or disappear.

Attitude to adopt
You must make things develop, transform them, reappraise them, and allow your impulsiveness to express itself. Get rid of what you can no longer bear. Act with courage, even at the risk of shocking those around you.

If your question requires a "yes" or "no" answer: This response should be probably be taken as "no."

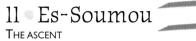

11 • Es-Soumou
THE ASCENT

12 • Es-Souqout
THE REVERSED

Symbol
This is a picture of warm air rising. It expresses success, fame, protection, fortune, power, honors, gratitude, growth, and development.

Meaning
The idea contained in this figure is goodness in all its manifestations. Joie de vivre, optimism, good health and the like… it is a very positive draw that promises satisfaction.

Attitude to adopt
This result foretells success through discipline, work, and good will. Your thoughts are positive and constructive, and they will lead you to success.

If your question must be answered with a "yes" or a "no": The answer is an emphatic "yes."

Symbol
This figure refers to the heaviness of earth and expresses melancholy, discouragement, renunciation, lassitude, fear, dark, negative thoughts, scruples, regrets, and isolation.

Meaning
The idea contained here is sadness and lack of motivation. There is hostility or withdrawal on the part of people around you. You are faced with problems that trouble you and to which you see no solution.

Attitude to adopt
Your troubles arise from the fear of doing wrong or not measuring up. Don't brood over your problems, don't let them affect those around you, and don't think the worst of situations. This sadness wants only to disappear.

If your question must be answered with a "yes" or a "no": This figure says "no."

13 ● Er-Ribh
ACQUISITION

Symbol
This figure symbolizes the water of the oceans and rivers and represents increase, growth, fertility, abundance, generosity, ambition, benevolence, and moral sense.

Meaning
Er-Ribh heralds improvement. Financial acquisitions, financial investment, purchases, and profits: in particular it involves material enrichment. It is a phase of progress and development.

Attitude to adopt
The time is favorable if you remain honest and sincere. Be careful not to denigrate anyone, to judge others falsely, or to keep for yourself alone the benefit you may gain from the situation.

If your question must be answered with a "yes" or a "no": The answer is "yes."

14 ● El-Khousâra
LOSS

Symbol
This results pictures cold air that blows hard. It suggests running away from things, lack of foresight, fickleness, instability, injustice, and deception.

Meaning
You are faced with diminishment and constraint. You may lose all that you own, flee from a situation, squander gains, or be clumsy towards others. A relationship is losing meaning; a person or situation is escaping you.

Attitude to adopt
In this unfavorable situation, you will be misunderstood, and your enterprise may be doomed to fail. You must get an idea out of your mind or get rid of someone, reconsider the situation, and regain your confidence. Then you can start again.

If you question must be answered with a "yes" or a "no": The answer is "no."

15 ● El-Liqâ
THE ENCOUNTER

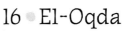

16 ● El-Oqda
LIMITATION

Symbol
This figure represents rainwater and expresses what is suddenly brought together, either in partnership or in opposition. It speaks of an agreement or a disagreement, a duality, or a change of opinion.

Meaning
Depending on your situation, look for an encounter, a rendezvous, an exchange of ideas or, on the other hand, tension and confrontation.

Attitude to adopt
Be open to others, try and communicate. Be aware that everything that aims to bring people together, to get to know others better, is positive, but don't rule out unforeseen circumstances!

If your question must be answered with a "yes" or a "no": This reading is favorable but does not provide a "yes" or "no" answer.

Symbol
This figure conjures up air filled with mist and expresses immobilization, difficulties, isolation, work, responsibilities, prudence, and duty.

Meaning
Expect solitude, whether deliberate or unintentional, a temporary difficulty that forces you to stabilize the situation or stand your ground. El-Oqda indicates restrictions, an obstacle that must be overcome, a task that must be accomplished, or work that requires perseverance and concentration.

Attitude to adopt
You seem unable to get the situation to evolve. Indeed, to do so requires time, effort, and sacrifices. Move forward on this craggy path with patience and determination. Soon the way will become smoother.

If your question must be answered with a "yes" or "no": The answer is "no."

The Tarot

No one knows by whom, where or when the Tarot was created. In Europe it was first discovered in the mid-fifteenth century in Italy, where Bonifacio Bembo painted the figures used on the cards on the occasion of a marriage between the Visconti and Sforza families. In the eighteenth century Antoine Court de Gébelin discovered the *Book of Thoth-Hermes Trismegistus*, which was said to contain the universal knowledge of the Egyptian priests. In the nineteenth century, Eliphas Levi compared the tarot to Kabbalah and explained the correspondence between the arcana and the 22 letters of the Hebrew alphabet. In the twenty-first century its mysterious arcana contain symbols, images, and messages that still must be interpreted.

Reading the tarot cards

Choose a quiet place where you will not be disturbed. You should be aware that it is preferable to read the Tarot for someone else rather than yourself. The cards described here are the twenty-two trumps making up the major arcana. The fifty-six other cards, the minor arcana, are not dealt with here.

- If you have a set of Tarot cards, shuffle them, ask the other person to cut the cards with their left hand, spread the cards face down in an arc of a circle, and then to choose three cards.
- **If you do not have a set of Tarot cards, use the following method:**

1
Choose three numbers between 11 and 21 and write them down.

2
Put your finger on one of the twenty-two cards at random and count the first number you chose, clockwise or counterclockwise as you wish, round the circle of cards. This gives you your first card: write its name down.

3
Put your finger on the card you have landed on and count the second number you chose, round the circle of cards, again clockwise or counterclockwise as you wish. This will give you a second card: write its name down.

4
Repeat the operation with the third number to obtain the third card.

You have now identified three cards.
The first card talks about the situation, the assets, and the hopes of the questioner.

The second card talks about conditions external to the questioner, about other people, and the handicaps and the obstacles that the questioner may encounter.

The third card is the result. It gives the message, what lies in store, and the answer to the question.

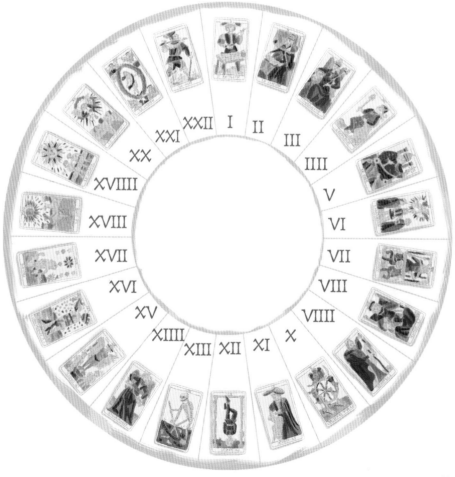

Interpretations

I • The Magician

A DYNAMIC, ENTERPRISING YOUNG MAN
WITH ALL THE OPPORTUNITIES OF SUCCESS
IN HIS HANDS

Symbol
The Magician announces new beginnings, encounters, opportunities, or
another path to follow.

As the first card
You are full of initiative and joie de vivre.
You want to change things, to find things
out, and to experiment. Your assets are
your enthusiasm, ambition, health, vitality, and creativity, and your ability to adapt
to new situations.

As the second card
There is nothing to fear except for a
slight lack of concentration, indecision,
and confusion because the situation is
not as clear as you think. There is duplicity, lying and grandstanding on the part
of others.

As the third card
You can be confident. Something is about
to start, and it is very positive: a pleasant
surprise, a romantic encounter, easy
communication, or creativity in work. Be
optimistic, brave, and bold; follow your
impulses and take decisions or risks. You
can have an influence on events and elsewhere. It is up to you to set things in
motion.

II • The High Priestess

A WOMAN ON WHOM YOU CAN RELY.
WISE, ERUDITE, AND PEACEFUL, SHE IS A
RELIABLE GUIDE.

Symbol

Shy, secretive, and undemonstrative, the High Priestess promises lasting good fortune as long as things are not rushed.

As the first card

You calmly await developments. You know things will happen gradually and lead you to success. Maternal or conjugal love may be involved. You may have a task to perform or something to teach others.

As the second card

There is nothing serious to fear except for some delays, a little coolness, and a lack of enthusiasm and imagination. Feelings are hidden and not easily expressed. There is a task that requires patience and determination.

As the third card

The situation will develop slowly but surely. There will be preparatory work, an initiation, a peaceful and faithful union, a realization, a pregnancy or an apprenticeship. You will benefit from the help of someone older than you. Be patient, honest, and intuitive. Don't overanalyze; listen to yourself.

III · The Empress

SMILING AND WELL-SITUATED, THE EMPRESS
RULES OVER THE INTELLECTUAL WORLD
AND DOMINATES THE MALE SEX.

Symbol
The Empress rules with an iron fist in a
velvet glove.

As the first card
Determined and ambitious, you want to
bring an important project to a successful conclusion and develop intellectually
or materially. This card is more spiritual
than sentimental, making you lucid and
dynamic. Remain independent and
truthful in all circumstances.

As the second card
If you are a woman you may dominate
your partner or put your ambition
before your emotions. If you are a man,
you are submissive to female influence,
sexually and emotionally dependent.

As the third card
Success is certain if you stand firm, take
decisions and act on them. There is the
dominant influence of a woman (mother, wife…), material progress, social promotion, academic success, marriage, and
pregnancy. You are promised success,
expansion, and creativity.

IIII •The Emperor

THE EMPEROR KNOWS WHAT HE WANTS.
WITH KINGLY AUTHORITY HE DOMINATES
THE SITUATION.

Symbol
Male energy, power, and virility. He has an authoritarian character but is also a protector.

As the first card
This card deals with ambition, power, and energy. You have the strength and determination to make the situation develop, make a conquest, and achieve a tangible result. An important decision must be taken, but it is up to you to channel your energies, gather people together, and guide them.

As the second card
Be careful not to be domineering, narrow-minded, brusque, or intransigent. A little flexibility, delicacy, and diplomacy would not go amiss. Otherwise people might resent your power and rebel. Possibly a man (father, husband, boss…) is overshadowing you or restricting you.

As the third card
Success is certain, if passion does not take precedence over reason. This card speaks of riches, health, good news, stability, and responsibilities. Show respect for established customs, look for the support of an influential person, make a decision but remain honest, loyal, and law-abiding.

V • The Pope

THE POPE IS OLD AND WISE; HE HAS
EXPERIENCE OF THINGS AND OF PEOPLE. HE
IS A HELP AND A SUPPORT.

Symbol
The Pope possesses integrity, patience,
and balance. He sets an example that you
can follow.

As the first card
Your assets include inspiration, wisdom,
kindness, and generosity. It is a matter of
sharing your experience, giving guidance
and being interested in others in order to
help them and encourage them to develop. Your role is to patiently pass on your
knowledge.

As the second card
There are no pitfalls to be afraid of, apart
from a few delays, some inertia or laziness. Do not be intolerant and, in particular, do not hold grudges. You must find
common ground, remain honest, be
loyal, set an example, forgive, and accept
forgiveness.

As the third card
Do not look for immediate success. It is
guaranteed as long as you join forces
with others, concentrate on the essential, and guard against impatience, violence and temptation. You are close to
achieving equilibrium, a new stability if
you listen to what people are trying to
tell you. Conciliation, help, and leniency
will lead to success.

VI • The Lover
HE HESITATES, HE WAVERS…
WHICH WAY WILL HE CHOOSE?

Symbol
The Lover stands at a crossroads. He is tempted by ease, beauty, and infidelity.

As the first card
This card speaks of a friendship, an association, an encounter, a relationship or a union. But it might also augur a separation. You are at a crossroads, and you are torn between the promise of pleasure and the voice of reason, between happiness stretching its arms towards you and the illusions of happiness. In other words, you do not know which way to turn…

As the second card
Look out for infidelity, fickleness, and indecision. You are dealing with a deceitful person, an ambiguous situation, a promise not kept, and jealousy. Perhaps you lack maturity or are giving in to ease and carelessness.

As the third card
Here you are on the threshold of a love story or an association. Everything will go smoothly, if you make an immediate choice, if you are honest towards the other person but also towards yourself. But be aware that the best way will be the most difficult, the one that demands effort.

VII •The Chariot

Symbol

The Chariot heralds a battle to be fought, a bold venture to be undertaken, a positive change, or a journey.

As the first card

You have the dynamism, vitality, and enthusiasm necessary to achieve success in your endeavors as well as control of yourself and therefore of events. The Chariot speaks of movement, progress, and realization… this is certainly a good start!

As the second card

The Chariot is a very positive card, and you have nothing to fear, apart perhaps from a little overwork, stress, too much ambition, confidence in yourself or optimism that might blind you.

As the third card

The Chariot replies "yes!" You will achieve success, overcome obstacles, and progress along your chosen path. It predicts a rewarding journey, an encounter, a marriage, a cure, progress, a promotion, an unexpected change, or an end to deadlock. A battle must be fought, but the result will justify your efforts.

VIII • Justice

ARMED WITH SWORD AND SCALES, JUSTICE
WEIGHS THE PROS AND CONS. WHICH WAY
WILL THE SCALES TIP?

Symbol

Justice speaks of an equilibrium that must
be found or maintained, a discipline to be
followed, or a just reward.

As the first card

This card prompts you to put your life
in order, see the various aspects of the
problem and differentiate good from
evil. A period of harmony is coming.
There may be an encounter, but before
this happens you must impartially look
at your own faults and qualities and those
of others.

As the second card

Justice as the second card underlines a
problem that may be of a social or sentimental nature, unless you are the vic-
tim of injustice or have committed an
error of judgment.

As the third card

Justice predicts a reward, a period of
peace and stability, a new relationship,
marriage, a wanted pregnancy, the pur-
chase of a house, or academic success.
It is time to make a dramatic decision and
view the situation in a more practical
way. Guard against passion and uncon-
trolled desires, and everything will be
well.

VIIII • The Hermit

THE HERMIT MAY BE OLD BUT HE IS WISE!
ALONE, HE WALKS SLOWLY IN SEARCH OF
TRUTH.

Symbol

Reflection, meditation, modesty, and prudence are the attributes of the Hermit.
Time is his master.

As the first card

You need time for solitude and self-
examination. You are searching for an
ideal, for the essential. You have a tendency to cut yourself off from the material world and to look inside yourself for
the answers to your questions. You are
hiding your own value or avoiding contact with others.

As the second card

Is it pride, selfishness or sadness? Whatever it may be, you seem to be distrust-
ful, your health is suffering, and either a
relationship no longer satisfies you or a
job no longer makes you happy. You
know you must change things, but for the
moment you are turning inwards.

As the third card

Do not look here if you are in search of
public success, passion or immediate satisfaction. The Hermit asks you to stand
back, take the time to think, listen to others, and to give good advice. If you persevere, if you are loyal, patient and
prudent, you will go far. Soon an important aspect of the situation will be
revealed, and you will discover another
facet of yourself.

X • The Wheel of Fortune

IT'S A LOTTERY! IT GOES UP, IT GOES
DOWN... THE WHEEL GOES ROUND!

Symbol

This card represents life with its ups and
downs, the eternal alternation of the
positive and the negative.

As the first card

You seem to be irritated, excited, and
shaken up. Your life is fast-paced and ever
changing, and your situation is unstable.
You are beginning a new chapter in your
life. You are trying to develop, to move on
to something else, or to behave differently.

As the second card

There is an obstacle, a pitfall, or a weakness that is delaying you. You have the
impression of stagnating or regressing.
You are shaken by unexpected news or
circumstances that are not yet favorable.

As the third card

A new deal, a new cycle... there is going
to be a change. If you were at "the top,"
you may expect to fall down, while if you
were at "the bottom," be prepared to
climb back up. This can be a time of
progress, an opportunity, a happy coin-
cidence, the end of your problems. Laziness and thoughtlessness would cause
your ruin; only effort and determination
will enable you to act.

XI ● Strength

A PRETTY WOMAN OVERCOMES THE
SAVAGE, DESTRUCTIVE INSTINCTS OF A
LION. SHE RULES ITS PASSIONS.

Symbol

This figure represents inner strength, that which gives you victory over yourself and consequently over events.

As the first card

You want to obtain something that appears difficult at first sight. There is a conquest that must be made, a competition, a beautiful ambition or a noble cause that must be defended. In this quest your best assets are activity, vitality, and independence, but especially the courage that will enable you to face all your problems.

As the second card

Pride, selfishness, and incomprehension… you lack gentleness, sensitiveness, and perhaps love. You are impatient, too ambitious or badly equipped to face the problems that might arise. Guard against laziness but also stress.

As the third card

A beautiful omen for the future! It predicts an encounter, a union, an engagement, an imminent marriage, a birth, academic honors, a promotion, commercial success, the winning of a competition, an exciting project. Act on your own, be determined and methodical, and you will succeed because your heart is pure.

XII • The Hanged Man

THIS IS A VERY UNCOMFORTABLE
POSITION… YET THE HANGED MAN
APPEARS AT EASE, RELAXED, AND SERENE.

Symbol

The Hanged Man heralds a transition, a kind of suspended animation that will allow your projects to ripen..

As the first card

You are completely undecided. You have chosen a different path from others, one that is more difficult because you are looking for truth, for an ideal in life. Selfless and badly equipped for the fight and challenge of competition, you feel alone, misunderstood, and powerless, and you fear that might have to sacrifice something.

As the second card

You are experiencing sadness, remorse, bitterness or obstacles. A project is being called into question, feelings of love are not shared, and a break-up, either temporary or final, is in the air. Unless you refuse to accept the situation or reject the break that appears to be inevitable?

As the third card

You are going through a transitional phase. Therefore, stand back, remain calm and patient, and do not lose heart even if the objective appears distant. Depending on the situation, the Hanged Man heralds a recovery, a birth, or a secret love.

XIII • Death

FEAR NOT, THIS CARD SPEAKS NOT OF
PHYSICAL DEATH BUT OF
TRANSFORMATION.

Symbol

Everything dies, and everything is reborn.
The end of one thing is the beginning of
another…

As the first card

Your situation is difficult, because you
have reached a turning point. A change,
perhaps even an upheaval, has taken
place, or you have experienced a separation. Remember defeat can be prof-
itable, a necessary change that will be
followed by a renewal.

As the second card

A project has not been successfully completed, you are facing an obstacle, you
lack self-confidence, a break-up is
announced, or perhaps a passion has
died. Accept the fact that you can no
longer live as you did before.

As the third card

A new phase, new love, new work or a
new period in your life… you are going
to change your behavior and your way
of life. This will not be easy, but it will
prove very beneficial. You are on the
threshold of a rebirth. Do not fear it,
welcome it!

XIIII ●Temperance

AN ANGEL, A SPIRIT BELONGING MORE TO
HEAVEN THAN TO EARTH, DECANTS PURE,
CELESTIAL WATER.

Symbol

Temperance expresses moderation. It speaks of communication, exchanges, and peace.

As the first card

Improvement, development, and regeneration… you want to become part of something bigger than yourself, to transform yourself in order to achieve equilibrium. Yes, the conditions are favorable, but you are fragile, and you must first resolve your own contradictions.

As the second card

Temperance is not a negative card. You may simply be a little unstable and vulnerable from a physical or psychological point of view. Just don't yield too easily to outside influences, or let yourself go.

As the third card

The omen is positive. You will attain equilibrium and harmony, you will strengthen a relationship, improve friendships or effect a reconciliation. This may also be reflected in a union, a recovery, new friendships, a positive unexpected event or a birth. Do not rush anything; everything will happen in due course.

XV • The Devil

A LITTLE FRIGHTENING AT FIRST SIGHT BUT
DO NOT LET THIS MISLEAD YOU... HE
HIDES AN UNSUSPECTED STRENGTH:
YOURS!

Symbol

The world of the Devil is a temporal one. His world is that of sex, money, and power.

As the first card

Driven by passion, you yearn for physical happiness, material and social success, or to conquer the object of your desires through force if need be. That is, unless you feel shackled to something or someone? In that case you will be able to find a way out.

As the second card

Lies, unhappy sexual experiences, bad people around you, excesses, lack of scruples, fraud, temptation, enemies, dependence on a person or a situation... fight your baser instincts, and do not give in to destructive thoughts.

As the third card

The Devil predicts a favorable situation in the material and physical fields: daring, courage, magnetism, health, vitality, money, sensual attraction, creative force or passionate sexual relationship. Be careful, you might become ensnared by this.

XVI •
The Tower
A SHOT ACROSS THE BOW, AN ALARM
SIGNAL... THIS CARD IS A WARNING

Symbol
This represents the destruction of false values and ways of life that are no longer acceptable.

As the first card
You are going through a troubled phase in your life, experiencing a difficult and controversial situation, or you are suffering from a trauma. You are having to reappraise yourself, you have discovered a truth, you have opened your eyes. It is a beneficial storm, a constructive ordeal, or a salutary crisis.

As the second card
After a financial, professional or emotional failure, your ego has suffered, and you have lost face. The fault lies not with others but with yourself, your pride, your selfishness, or your excessive ambition. There is a lesson you have not understood, and you have made mistakes. You need to change course.

As the third card
Warning! You must make a clean sweep and break with the past, even if it means taking risks and launching yourself into a new adventure. Depending on your question, this will be a beneficial break, a move, or another professional orientation. A radical change is on the horizon, but before this happens you must destroy in order to rebuild.

XVII ● The Star

THIS IS THE LUCKY STAR, THE ONE THAT
PROTECTS YOU…

Symbol

The Star speaks of good fortune, hope,
inspiration, or credit for something from
the past that is at last bringing its
reward.

As the first card

Your situation is good, even excellent.
The time is favorable and opportunities
for happiness abound. You have talent,
artistic gifts, imagination, healthy aspirations, and the ability to create something
beautiful and new.

As the second card

The Star is a very positive card. You
should expect no major difficulties,
although you might be a bit too easy-
going or become prey to shamelessness,
dreaming, self-indulgence, or a little confusion. It may speak of a desire that has
not yet been fulfilled.

As the third card

Do not worry, the Star heralds harmony, peace, safety, spiritual and romantic
love, an encounter with your soul mate,
the end of your ordeals, a recovery, a creative action, or a birth… You have a brilliant future ahead of you; do not let
negative thoughts stand in you way.

XVIII • The Moon
THE MOON REGULATES OUR NIGHTS, LIGHT OR DARK, INHABITED BY DREAMS OR GHOSTS

Symbol
Indicating imagination, sensitivity, and receptivity, this card also speaks of introspection, illusion, and nostalgia.

As the first card
Hypersensitive, for the moment you are living on an emotional plane. Events linked to the past weigh upon you, and you fear something that may or may not happen. You have doubts. If the situation involves the home, children, or an artistic project, you are on the right path.

As the second card
Misunderstanding, lies, unproductive memories, lack of realism or an error of judgment: you are kidding yourself, your situation is blurred, you are disappointed by someone, or you are becoming withdrawn.

As the third card
You will have to face your fears, shake off the past, and get back to basics. But instability is threatening. Regarding relationships, you must remain clear-headed. This card speaks of deceit, illusion, or deception. Be prudent and develop your character.

XVIIII • The Sun

THE SUN OBLITERATES DARK FORCES. IT IS
THE VICTORY OF DAY OVER NIGHT. ALL
OBSTACLES ARE REMOVED.

Symbol

The Sun brings illumination, distributes
love and happiness, and opens the heart
and mind to life.

As the first card

Your situation is good, and your assets
are numerous. You have plenty of ambition. You want to shine, succeed, build,
undertake a project, love a partner or
children, or generously help those
around you. You are on the road to satisfaction.

As the second card

The Sun does not have negative conno-
tations, although it's best to guard against
pride, playing to the gallery or bluffing.
Moderate your ambition and excessive
self-confidence. Do not hide the truth
from yourself.

As the third card

A very beautiful omen! The Sun promises love, joy, an encounter, marriage, a
happy sex life, a birth, good health, success, fame, the recognition of one's talents, artistic success, financial gains, help,
a solution to life's problems…

XX •Judgment

THE TRUMPETS OF THE LAST JUDGMENT
AWAKEN THE CONSCIENCE. IT IS A REBIRTH,
A DISCOVERY, A RENEWAL.

Symbol
Judgment heralds the end of an ordeal, a second chance, or the clarification of a situation.

As the first card
Leaving the cold and darkness, you emerge into full light. Your situation involves a change, a sudden and unexpected event, dynamism, and overexcitement. You are given the opportunity to be reborn, to start again.

As the second card
A problem has been only half solved, a piece of news has shaken you, you are experiencing legal problems, you are indecisive, disappointed, stressed, you have a bad opinion of yourself, or perhaps you must forgive someone or let something go.

As the third card
A verdict will be rendered, and you will see your situation in a new light. One door closes, but another opens. Now comes the settlement of an old problem, the reward for your efforts, a moment of truth, regained health, the realization of project dear to your heart, the birth of a long-awaited child, or the end of an ordeal.

XXI • The World

ANGELS, ANIMALS AND HUMANS ARE
GATHERED IN THIS CARD ... IT IS THE
APOTHEOSIS!

Symbol

The World expresses the Whole. It
speaks of material and spiritual accom-
plishments.

As the first card

You are on the way, you are evolving. Your
situation is about to develop and take off,
and your horizon is about to broaden.
You are ready to move, to travel, to discover the world at large, and to experience new, unknown sensations.

As the second card

The World against you means a lot of
effort for very little result; it means scat-
tering, idleness, a tendency to laxity or a
lack of concentration. You must expect
material limitations and accept yourself
as you are.

As the third card

A very beautiful omen... The world is
your oyster! You will experience success,
overcome obstacles, travel abroad, discover new horizons, your merits will be
recognized, you will start a new adventure, transform your image, and fulfill
your wishes. Fear nothing; on the contrary, you should rejoice!

The Fool

THIS CARD HAS NO NUMBER, NO HOUSE, AND NO DIRECTION... THE FOOL IS IN SEARCH OF AN IDENTITY.

Symbol

Drifting here and there, the Fool takes you anywhere and shows you the worst as well as the best.

As the first card

You situation is unstable. You are wandering right and left, buffeted by events or caught in a rhythm that escapes you. In search of something or someone, you are finding it difficult to adapt to the world around you or to choose an objective.

As the second card

Guard against an excessively carefree attitude, eccentricity, and infidelity. Your projects are chaotic, incoherent or illusory, and you allow yourself to be pushed by circumstances. You lack rigor and are not practical, or you try to escape from your responsibilities. Control your instincts, become aware of reality, and remain reasonable.

As the third card

There is a change in your mood. A new project, an unexpected move, a search for freedom, a journey, an original adventure or experience, an opportunity to be seized with both hands or a brainstorm... This card does not speak of material, professional or romantic success but, depending on the other cards drawn, it speaks of spiritual development, restless wandering or renewed awareness.

Tonalamalt

The Aztec Book of Destiny

Astrology and divination played a major part in Aztec civilization. To predict the future, the priests—the *tonalpouhques*, "those who count the signs"—interpreted the calendar of 260 days known as the *tonalpoualli*, a complex system of sacred numbers. They studied the cycles of the sun, the moon, and Venus, and interpreted them in relation to the *tonalli*, the twenty symbols of the calendar.

Consulting the oracle

The symbols include mammals (deer, rabbit, dog, ocelot, monkey), reptiles (alligator, snake, lizard), and birds (vulture, eagle), as well as the elements (water, rain, wind). Added to these there are death, closely linked to the earth in Aztec thought, and movement, a reflection of solar and cosmic dynamics. Then there are also the three signs symbolizing the plant world (the grass, the reed and the flower), a sign for the mineral world (flint), and one for cultural aspects (the house).

1

Ask a question silently or ask the person you are consulting to ask the question in the same way.

2

Place your finger at random on one of the twenty tonalli of the wheel opposite and count thirteen squares clockwise or counter-clockwise as you wish.

3

The tonalli that you land on gives the answer to the question. Read its message and its prediction.

Interpretations

1 ● Cipactli
THE ALLIGATOR

In Aztec tradition, the alligator, a terrestrial animal, was thrown into the water by the soothsayers, thus starting the evolution of time. Symbol of primordial water, it represents childbirth and beginnings.

Omen

Excellent. It promises prosperity and even abundance if you care about work well done and become thoroughly involved in the situation that presents itself.

A favorable draw for planning work, starting a project, starting from scratch, creating an association, starting a relationship, or deciding to have a child.

An unfavorable draw for stabilizing a situation, turning back, completing a business deal or resolving a family problem.

2 ● Eecatl
THE WIND

The Aztec temples dedicated to the Wind had only curved walls because the Wind does not like right angles, and consequently, the clear-cut aspects of life.

Omen

Indecision, ambiguity, and instability… your enthusiasm is short-lived, and your desires are changing.

A favorable draw for everything concerning communication, ingenuity, fantasy, art, brief romantic relationships, changes of lifestyle, casual friendships, and traveling.

An unfavorable draw for lasting romantic relationships, clear-cut decisions, responsibilities, financial gains, and work that requires concentration and perseverance.

3 Calli
THE HOUSE

The House symbolizes the family, traditions, resistance to change, and the need for shelter against the stresses of life.

Omen
You must be prudent and persevering. This requires effort on your part, sacrifices, patience, and a very clear approach to the problem.

A favorable draw for everything relating to the home and family, concern for others, easing a conflict, following tradition or a clear-cut path, living in solitude, resting, and looking after oneself.

An unfavorable draw for everything relating to the social world, launching a new enterprise, starting a new love affair, following an original path or taking immediate action.

4 Cuetzpallin
THE LIZARD

Lively, smart, and effective, the Lizard never hurts itself even when it falls, and it catches its prey without effort… these things come to it naturally.

Omen
Excellent, as long as you guard against nervousness, laxness, lack of concentration, opportunism, and indifference to others.

A favorable draw for undertaking a daring or original project, working quickly and well, regaining your health, influencing others, accomplishing something important, or having an intense sexual relationship.

An unfavorable draw for family relationships, romantic friendships, settling a conflict, following others, or stabilizing a situation.

5 • Coatl
THE SERPENT

Like the "Plumed Serpent," the god of plant abundance, the Serpent indicates transformation.

Omen

Prosperity and good fortune, as long as you are worthy of it. If not, destiny could turn out to be adverse…

A favorable draw for following an idea through, concluding a project, gathering information, taking risks, transforming a situation, or changing your lifestyle, partner or work.

An unfavorable draw for resting on one's laurels, maintaining the status quo of a situation, standing one's ground, resolving disputes, revealing a secret or being satisfied with what one has.

6 • Miquiztli
DEATH

In the Aztec tradition, the symbol of death is not a bad omen. It calls upon us to concentrate on the deeper meaning of people and things, rather than on external aspects.

Omen

Good fortune but fragile. Do not trust passion and exaltation. Reflection, tranquility, and prudence are recommended.

A favorable draw for answering fundamental questions, undertaking a difficult task or one that requires time, accepting a lesser professional role, or winning someone's trust.

An unfavorable draw for accepting a leading post, traveling, getting excited about a love affair, becoming interested in a project or a person, acting lightly, or taking risks.

7 • Mazatl
THE DEER

The Deer was the most prized prey of Aztec hunters. Fast and with great stamina, it is constantly on the move but never strays far from its fellow creatures.

Omen
Encounters, contacts, meetings, traveling, and the discovery of new horizons.

A favorable draw for looking elsewhere for what you are lacking, enjoying a change of scene, finding family harmony, carrying out an artistic project, sharing love, sensuality, and sexuality, and living peacefully surrounded by friends or relatives.

An unfavorable draw for social advancement, taking command, dominating others, acting independently, leaving one's friends and family or following a routine in love or at work.

8 • Tochtili
THE RABBIT

The Rabbit, who likes eating more than working, was the symbol of the pleasure seeker in Aztec tradition.

Omen
Charming, engaging, and elusive, the Rabbit represents laxness, infidelity, and self-indulgence.

A favorable draw for having fun, taking risks, playing with people and situations, friendships, outings, communication, short-term relationships, sensual indulgence, and everything that involves pleasure.

An unfavorable draw for everything that requires effort, patience, endurance, lasting relationships, loyalty to a cause or a person, material gains, or social promotion.

9 • Atl
WATER

Indispensable to life, the symbol of Water is ambiguous. It expresses fertility but also anxiety because water can flood fields.

Omen
Water represents what is unpredictable: changing situations, versatile people, the ups and downs of life.

A favorable draw for resolving situations with emotional aspects, romantic relationships, passionate love affairs, or anything that involves imagination and creativity.

An unfavorable draw for stabilizing a situation, starting a project, making long-term plans, or solving a material, financial or practical problem.

10 • Itzcuintli
THE DOG

When someone died, the Aztecs sacrificed a dog so that it could accompany the dead person on the journey underground.

Omen
A fertile sign and a good omen, the dog represents loyalty, honesty, and generosity. It never abandons the person it loves.

A favorable draw for guiding others, helping, working as a team within a group, giving gifts, starting a lasting affair based on sincerity, or planning the birth of a child.

An unfavorable draw for short-term projects, asserting one's autonomy, working on one's own, acting as a leader, or giving in to the passion of the moment or to an infidelity.

11 ● Ozomatli
THE MONKEY

In Aztec tradition it was the Monkey who accidentally invented fire and gave it to human beings. He symbolizes inventiveness and the unexpected.

Omen
Rather good but changeable. Surprises, fantasy, curiosity, affairs of the heart, and also ill-advised expenses.

A favorable draw for communicating, expressing your ideas, acting as intermediary, undertaking a short-term project, having fun, partying, changing your partner, adapting to a new environment, or living freely.

An unfavorable draw for making an important decision that will commit you to the future, for starting a long-term relationship, making or investing money, being involved in a long-term project, or putting your trust in people.

12 ● Malinalli
GRASS

In Aztec tradition grass that dries out and then becomes green again expresses a crisis and a recovery, an end and a new beginning.

Omen
Contradictory indications depending on the current situation. If the situation is good, it may get worse; if it is bad it may improve.

A favorable draw for dreaming, regaining one's physical or mental strength, getting out of a painful or complex situation, starting over, finding peace after a tense period. Acting kindly, tactfully, and sensitively will prove beneficial.

An unfavorable draw for stabilizing a situation or a relationship, planning the birth of a child, making long-term commitments, setting oneself an objective in the distant future, relying on luck, or acting right away.

13 ● Acatl
THE REED

The reed symbolizes luxurious vegetation. A sign of prestige, it represents learning, knowledge, and religion.

Omen

Excellent. It refers to the moral character that gives one power over events and authority over people.

A favorable draw for showing what you are worth, expressing your opinions, undertaking an intellectual project, making yourself popular, challenging yourself, or for becoming interested in spirituality and human nature.

An unfavorable draw if you hope to make material gains, invest, borrow money or you are about to become involved in a love affair. This is because the stem of the reed is hollow… it has no heart.

14 ● The Ocelot
THE OCELOT

The animal incarnation of the Sun in its nocturnal phase, this dangerous feline was feared by the Aztecs. A symbol of pride, nobility, and bravery, it also expresses aggressiveness, voracity, and instinctual drives.

Omen

New responsibilities, increased power, enthusiasm, and tenacity, this sign represents ambition but also confrontation or danger.

A favorable draw for carrying out grand designs, working efficiently, discovering a secret, engaging in a passionate love affair, starting a project, making people obey you, or having influence over others.

An unfavorable draw for giving in to idleness, maintaining the status quo, refusing responsibility, playing a secondary role, or asking yourself or someone else to be faithful.

15 • Quauhtli
THE EAGLE

Venerated for having conquered the darkness, the Eagle carried the newly created Sun to the zenith. It expresses lucidity, foresight, and perfectionism.

Omen
The Eagle leaves nothing to chance. It speaks of success that requires self-control, commitment, and perseverance.

A favorable draw for winning through force or legal action, taking risks, making decisions, anticipating a situation, saving money, undertaking a scientific or independent project, or charming and conquering a partner.

An unfavorable draw for becoming part of a team, mixing in a group, relying on chance, remaining dependent on a person or a situation, spending money, or letting things take their course.

16 • Cozcaquauhtli
THE VULTURE

"The Eagle with the necklace," as he was called by the Aztecs, is the symbol of wisdom, calm, and poise. He is the ancient sage dispensing guidance to those who need it.

Omen
The outcome of the situation is not in your hands. You must act sensibly and competently or ask the guidance of an experienced person.

A favorable draw for having talks, expressing your convictions, teaching or being taught, judging the actions of others, bringing up children, regaining your health, or living to a ripe old age.

An unfavorable draw for feeling independent, starting a love affair, indulging in sensuality and passion, or acting rashly or on a whim.

17 • Ollin
MOVEMENT

Ollin is the name of the rubber used by the Aztecs to make balls for playing games with. By multiplying the force transmitted to it, Ollin expresses dynamic action.

Omen
Good fortune and happiness, as long as you are serious about your goals. What matters here is to use one's will, make sustained efforts, and keep on moving.

A favorable draw for everything that involves intellectual pursuits, responsibilities, noble sentiments, long-term projects, friendly relationships, journeys, business trips, or aesthetic and artistic development.

An unfavorable draw for acting as leader, slackening one's efforts, relaxing, refusing to move on, acquiring material goods, or borrowing money.

18 • Tecpat
FLINT

The flint knife was used in human sacrifices for cutting out the hearts of vanquished warriors to feed the Sun. Symbol of toughness and austerity, it does not allow room for fantasy.

Omen
This symbol is about taking up a challenge, about the courage, honesty, and moral rectitude needed in the situation that is worrying you.

A favorable draw for seeking honors, assuming responsible positions, sacrificing yourself for a good cause, for social and professional relationships and decisions, and actions that require practicality, seriousness, and clarity.

An unfavorable draw for family or sentimental relationships, sloppiness, relaxation, fantasy, indecision, journeys and pleasure trips, or light or frivolous situations.

19 Quiauitl
RAIN

A symbol with many facets, Rain can be a benefactor, but it also can burst into a tempest or torrential downpour.

Omen
Here you are faced with a cause that may not be worth the trouble, youthful indiscretions, infatuation, or an urge that is as sudden as it is irrational.

A favorable draw for travel to distant places, meetings, falling in love, acting on impulse, love at first sight, outings, pleasures, and temptations of every kind.

An unfavorable draw for finding serenity and repose, or for works that require determination, enduring romantic attachments, acquisitions and financial investments.

20 Xochitl .
THE FLOWER

In the Aztec tradition, the flower, sensual and desirable, was a symbol of play, easy love, art, and beauty.

Omen
The Flower represents pleasure, dizziness, and excess. Guard against hopes and disillusionment because the Flower is fragile, wilting when it is touched.

A favorable draw for anything related to artistic pursuits (painting, theater, cinema, music, dance, and so on), to love (flirting, encounters, and seduction), and to pleasure trips.

An unfavorable draw for hard, difficult tasks that require effort and perseverance, for financial earnings, and social advancement. Avoid anything to do with gambling—you are certain to lose.

Colors

The predominant characteristic of color symbolism is its universality. Interpretations may vary according to different cultural areas, but colors will remain as supports of symbolism everywhere and for all time. This is the case with Tarot cards, in Greek, African, and Mayan mythology, in the Kabbalah, in astrology, in alchemy, and in the interpretation of dreams. Colors also correspond to different states of mind, such as passion, loyalty, tenderness or jealousy. They describe emotions and express feelings. Using the divinatory game presented here, you can put the colors of love into play day after day.

How to consult the oracle

1

Choose a number between 1 and 20 at random. Select a color on the color wheel opposite, and from there count the number you have chosen, clockwise or counterclockwise as you wish.

Note the color you land on. This color indicates the tenor of your romantic feelings.

2

Choose a second number between 1 and 20 at random. Put your finger back on the color you first started from, and from there count the second number you have chosen, clockwise or counter-clockwise as you wish.

3

Read the symbolism of each color, then the combination of the two colors to find out what characterizes your relationship today.

Colors

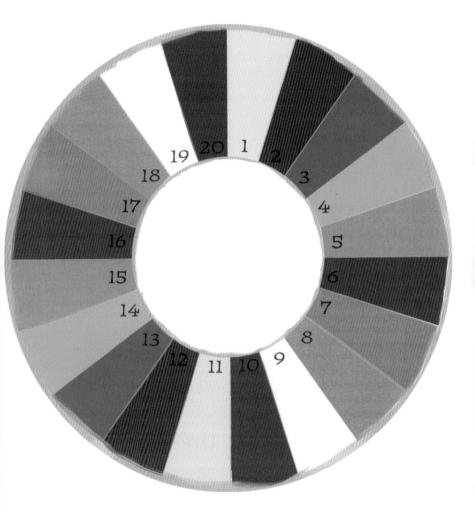

The ten colors

Yellow

This is the color of the sun, of gold, and of light. Yellow represents radiating love, filled with warmth and cheerfulness. Prepared to give of itself and to start or revive a story of love, it expresses generosity.

Omen
Capable of clarifying even the most confused situations, you are going to make them develop in a positive direction and communicate your feelings of love.
Attitude to adopt: It is time to take the initiative, to express yourself, and to say: I love you!

Red

The color of fire and blood, red symbolizes impulsive, immediate, total love. Red expresses passionate feelings, full of eagerness and desire. Red is the color of physical love, of sexual pleasure; it is a flame that burns itself out or devours and destroys.

Omen
There is no room for shyness or daydreaming. You have the strength to conquer, you are going to precipitate things or dominate your partner. There is energy or even provocation in the air!

Attitude to adopt: Do not hesitate, break with old habits and follow your impulses, but be careful not to go too far!

Blue

The color of the sky, blue represents open spaces, escape, and freedom. It symbolizes sincere, imaginative love, full of freshness. Spiritualized and idealized, such love can lose its passionate nature or become confused with friendship.

Omen
You will have the opportunity to enter into dialogue, make contacts, meet others, and even turn situations to your advantage. Today everything is possible!
Attitude to adopt: Do not remain in a rut. Change your direction and your timetable, think outside the box, and show some originality.

Green

The color of spring, youth, and romanticism, it fills you with hope and inspires you with music and poetry. But it can also take everything away in one fell swoop!

Omen

Green is the color of a carefree spirit, of a mind full of dreams and illusions. You may find your partner elusive and feel like escaping from reality. On the other hand, you may experience some magical moments!

Attitude to adopt: Do not pursue impossible or perfect love, but live each day to the full without thinking of yesterday or tomorrow.

Orange

Deeper than yellow but less violent than red, this color symbolizes balance and harmony in emotional relationships.

Omen

Orange promises growth, enjoyment of life and enthusiasm. You will experience strong, generous feelings. It is not just a flirtation or a simple encounter but a meeting that will lead to a long-term relationship.

Attitude to adopt: Commit yourself, become involved, take on responsibilities, agree to things… make a choice!

Violet

Representing spirituality and mysticism, this color, deeper than blue and calmer than red, speaks of intellectual love, peaceful and composed.

Omen

You are on the road to discovering profound, lasting love, friendlier and gentler rather than one purely physical or sensual. It may also involve an older person who has already experienced marriage or a partnership.

Attitude to adopt: Look at your situation from a distance and share your intellectual tastes. Commit your heart but also your mind to this relationship. Sexual pleasure is not the objective.

Pink

This color symbolizes tenderness, delicacy, charm, and beauty, but also voluptuousness, a distinct taste for pleasure in all its forms.

Omen

Seduction and sensuality will be present, but guard against fickleness, carelessness, or secrecy. Perhaps it involves a person who cannot live alone, who is capricious and dependent?

Attitude to adopt: Express your tenderness and your caresses but do not allow yourself to be influenced by the opinion of others or overcome by memories or illusions.

Gray

Between shade and dusk, halfway between lukewarm and cold, gray symbolizes neutrality, austerity, or stability.

Omen

Gray does not promise overwhelming enthusiasm but the search for equilibrium. It may also involve a secretive, thoughtful person who finds it difficult to express feelings.

Attitude to adopt: Your love needs time to express itself. You must wait for the right moment to act. For the time being, be at peace with yourself. If you do so, you will have a better chance of living happily with the other person.

White

White expresses innocence, modesty, purity, and virginity. Its ideal is noble, its fidelity is total, and its love almost inaccessible.

Omen

White expresses a lack of warmth and passion. It involves a person who has not yet been in love or is afraid to become so. But it may also indicate the promise of an encounter, a white sheet on which you will write your own love story…

Attitude to adopt: Don't act yet, and don't rush anything. Just be receptive, ready to welcome and share what may come to pass.

Brown

This color represents earth and everything that is fixed and tangible. Rather than enthusiasm or passion, it speaks of wisdom and shyness. It has a peaceful side but is slightly on the defensive.

Omen

This color refers to a thoughtful person who tries to build a solid foundation for love. Your feelings will evolve slowly but surely and will develop into a lasting relationship.

Attitude to adopt: Only sincere words and profound feelings will have a chance of thrilling your partner. Be tender and sincere; then the situation will gradually improve.

Color associations

Yellow and...

Yellow and yellow: Two suns. Your love is passionate or as dry as the desert. You illuminate each other, or you hide the truth from each other.

Yellow and red: Fire and light. Passion, a burning love, and torrid sensuality… peace will be made in bed or not at all.

Yellow and blue: Sun and blue sky. The weather is fine. This combination represents a bond, a friendship that turns into love or an extra-marital affair.

Yellow and green: Nature in the sunshine. A romantic love affair, a poetic declaration, or emotional revitalization, this combination indicates a fertile love.

Yellow and pink: A shining flower. A budding love, sweet nothings, presents… It is tender and sweet. But be careful and don't blunder!

Yellow and orange: Overflowing. All that the two partners want is beautiful perspectives, but watch out for promises not kept!

Yellow and violet: Sharing. This is not a passing infatuation but the opportunity to experience lasting, profound love.

Yellow and gray: Sun and clouds. One person expresses feelings, while the other holds back. Will the sun break through?

Yellow and white: Dazzling. You are on the road to ideal love, pure and unblemished. Lies, however insignificant, are inadvisable.

Yellow and brown: Warming up. In this complementary combination, love is expressed both physically and spiritually.

Red and...

Red and red: Violence. There is jealousy and aggression in the air. Guard against overindulgence!

Red and blue: Contrast. One lives the language of passion and raw desire, while the other speaks of ideas and freedom. You are not on the same wavelength.

Red and green: Complementing each other. Red is action and dynamism while green is gentleness and passivity. One partner provides the motivation; the other keeps things calm.

Red and orange: Energy. Orange brings harmony, balancing the passion of the red. The red carries it along unknown paths…

Red and violet: Strength and wisdom. Close to each other, these two colors combine enthusiasm and maturity. A beautiful combination.

Red and pink: Muted color. One is fully present, while the other is full of nuances. Who will make concessions?

Red and gray: Discrepancy. Differences in objectives or temperaments mean that this partnership will be difficult to sustain.

Red and white: All or nothing. Sexual pleasure or total abstinence? Passion or loyalty? You will have to find common ground.

Red and brown: A promised union. If brown remains on the defensive, red will grow tired of it. But if brown follows red, the couple will go far.

Blue and...

Blue and blue: The sky and space. Both of you dream of freedom. Today, favor friendship over love.

Blue and green: The sky and the sea. A sensual and spiritual union, with inspiration and imagination in common,

Blue and orange: Changes. Orange requires harmony, balance, and peace. Blue, on the other hand, loves renewal and freedom.

Blue and violet: A deep relationship. Close to one another, the couple loves journeys, discoveries, and fantasy.

Blue and pink: Boys and girls. A complementary combination. Blue provides idealism and pink tenderness.

Blue and gray: Blue sky, gray sky. Changeable weather, showers, lightning… each partner must remain spiritually independent.

Blue and white: Fraternity. There is common ground: the urge to live a love without limits, ideal, absolute…

Blue and brown: The sky and the earth. Brown is solid, practical, and grounded. Will brown follow blue so that they can create their own love story?

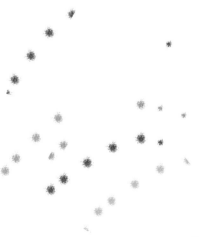

Green and...

Green and green: What are you striving for?... Youth, lack of concern or passivity... which one of the couple will point the way and make the decisions?

Green and orange: Mother Nature. With inspired love, affectionate harmony, warmth, and youthful feelings, this couple grows to love each other more every day.

Green and violet: Initiation. The freshness of green is allied with the maturity of violet. In this combination, the first must follow the second.

Green and pink: Youth. Lighthearted, whimsical, perhaps careless: this combination may lack strength or maturity.

Green and gray: The romanticism of the one fits badly with the austerity of the other, but at least it will be a calm and stable relationship.

Green and white: Liveliness. A new union or one that comes back to life... today anything is possible!

Green and brown: The vegetal world. In the image of nature, this is a promise of growth, fertility, and flowering.

Orange and...

Orange and orange: Two halves… The combination involves reunions and the promise of achieving balance, harmony, and unity.

Orange and violet: A beautiful mixture. The first person provides enthusiasm and the second maturity… together, they will go far.

Orange and pink: Fruit and flowers. Orange becomes involved in the relationship, wanting physical love, which should not alarm pink!

Orange and gray: Hot and cold. Into this mixture of light and shade, orange can bring out gray from its solitude, its gloom.

Orange and white: Encouraging. Both have pure feelings and the taste for balance, an idea raised up by love.

Orange and brown: Fertility. With warm sentiments, harmony, and accomplishment, the union is solid and concrete.

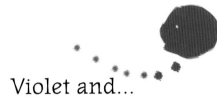

Violet and...

Violet and violet: Calm. The repetition of violet is more suitable for mature people than young lovers.

Violet and pink: Tenderness. Love is subtle. This association speaks of constancy, restraint, and self-mastery.

Violet and gray: Rather sad. It implies melancholy or boredom, unless there is assessment or self-examination to be carried out.

Violet and white: Idealism. Faith in eternal love, fidelity, a combination that is full of wisdom, beauty, and good feelings.

Violet and brown: Restraint. A combination of somber tones. Is freedom or the flame of desire missing here?

Pink and...

Pink and pink: Voluptuousness. An excessive taste for pleasure… It is good but each is overly dependent on the other.

Pink and gray: Pastel. An association in muted color for a union that is hard to enliven or to revive.

Pink and white: Dappled. An adolescent liaison that is in suspense, on the point of beginning or renewing itself.

Pink and brown: A flower of the earth. Pink may be let down by the material side of brown. Brown risks being offended up by the lightness of the pink.

Gray and...

Gray and gray: Patience. Neutrality, coolness, and solitude… this is an austere union or one that needs time to develop.

Gray and white: Colorless. They resemble each other. Putting aside some dark ideas.

Gray and brown: Rather boring. A stable, solid union, but one that struggles to take off or regenerate itself.

White and...

White and white: Virginal. Total, absolute, ideal love, but it may also remain… virgin.

White and brown: No overindulgence. A faithful, calm or reasonable union, unless one of the couple takes on the responsibilities of the other.

Brown and...

Brown and brown: Earth with earth. This is a creative love, which is good, but to give it wings the couple needs to be open to the world outside.

Zulu divination

Shells, nuts, grains of corn, stones or bones have just been thrown onto the ground . We are in South Africa, in the land of the Zulus. With "the people of the skies," it is the *sangoma* or witch doctor, the "soothsayer"—usually a woman—who interprets the signs and the omens. Traditionally, numbers have a primordial importance, and every one of them—up to one million—has a meaning.

Consulting the oracle

In the oracle presented here, only the numbers from 1 to 13 will be used to predict the future.

The oracle takes the numbers and associates them with symbols that relate to the questioner, the people surrounding the questioner, and the questioner's material well-being:

the **Warrior** represents the questioner;

the **Male** is a man the questioner is thinking of;

the **Female** is a woman the questioner is thinking of;

the **Chief** is the spiritual authority;

Cattle symbolize the material goods of the questioner.

Originally, the *sangoma* used monkey or crocodile bones. You can use flat stones or even matches instead.

The five symbols

the Warrior

the Male

the Female

the Chief

Cattle

1

With stones

Find eighteen flat stones. You will need thirteen stones numbered from 1 to 13; write the numbers on one of their faces. Draw the symbols on both sides of the remaining five stones.

With matches

Take eighteen matches. Write the numbers 1 to 13 (spelled out) on thirteen matches. The numbers should be written on one of the four faces of the match. Write the names of the five symbols on two sides of each of the five remaining matches.

2

Sit at a table. Take the eighteen matches or stones in one hand and ask your question. Blow on your hand, put your elbow on the table and open your hand, letting the matches or stones fall from the height of your forearm.

3

Add together all the visible numbers. The numbers on the sides or bottom are considered 'hidden' and are not taken into account.

4

If the total of the visible numbers comes to a number greater than 13, reduce it by adding the digits to each other (see example on next page) until the number is between 1 and 13 inclusive. Make a note of the total obtained.

5

Look and see if any of the symbols are touching numbers that are not hidden. If so, make a note of the associations.

6

Read the oracle that relates to the number found in step 4 as well as the symbol-number associations, where applicable, found in step 5.

Example

1 As a result of your throw, the visible numbers are 1, 5, 11, and 12. Add them: 1 + 5 + 11 + 12 = 29. 29 is greater than 13, so reduce it: 29, that is 2 + 9 = 11.

2 As a result of your throw, some symbols are touching the visible numbers: the Warrior is touching 11 and the Chief is touching 12.

3 To interpret the throw, simply read the text that relates to the number 11 and then the text of associations "11—Warrior" and "12—Chief."

If two or more numbers are touching a symbol, the numbers must be added together and reduced to a number between 1 and 13.

Interpretations

1 • Kunye

The number 1 is considered extremely beneficial by the Zulus. It is the number of the creation and symbolizes liberty. Its message is as follows: you must face up to the situation, motivate yourself, free yourself from attachment to things and to people, and look at the situation in a dispassionate manner. You must believe in yourself and in your abilities. Then, as long as your thoughts and actions are genuine, you will achieve success. You have the power to make decisions, and you are in charge. You should lead not follow. Don't let anyone influence you.

1 and the Warrior

Stop relying on others; make your own decisions. Like the Zulu warrior leaving for war, you must act alone, giving the best of yourself. In this way you will be victorious.

1 and the Male

This concerns a man with an original spirit who is hard to influence. If you want to associate yourself with him, you must show him that what you are achieving is good for both of you.

1 and the Female

Don't think that the woman in question here will follow you forever. You must also submit yourself to her demands. You will build a good relationship with her as long as you let her have enough space and freedom.

1 and the Chief

Even if you do not know him, do not see him, or do not want him; he offers you help. You are not alone. You simply have to open your heart and your spirit and accept the help that is offered.

1 and Cattle

An action decided on your part will enable you to acquire the material goods that please you. Don't count on other people. The omen is positive as long as you make an effort on your own.

2 ●Kubili

The number 2 represents imperfection and dissension. There are divergent opinions and differences in points of view. Dissension should be avoided by diplomacy and tact. This is not the moment to act strongly and in an individual manner but to follow others, to accept some dependency. Charm, friendship, pleasantness, and honesty will have a better chance of success than apathy, shyness, deceit, or treachery. This is a period of some obscurity. Your personal sun is not visible at this time, but you know that after the night, the sun will shine again.

2 and the Warrior

Your heart knows the correct response to the current situation of conflict. Don't push anyone into action, and don't wait for someone to follow you. Like the warrior, withdraw and wait for a better moment to attack again.

2 and the Male

This concerns a man with whom you should be cautious. Do not offend him, otherwise you will have to use a great deal of tact to calm the situation.

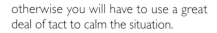

2 and the Female

This is a woman with whom you should be careful. It is not the moment to begin a relationship. Energetic action on your part would only serve to widen the gulf that separates you.

2 and the Chief

Don't look for answers to your questions outside yourself. Don't trust gurus, spiritual leaders, people who pretend to know more than you, or people to whom power seems important.

2 and Cattle

As to material goods, you are aiming too high, or the moment is not right. Know how to stop, not to acquire more. What you may gain now could quickly be lost.

3 Katatu

Because it cannot be divided in two, the number 3 is a very special one. It represents complementarity. Two women can quarrel but, if there is a third, she will bring their arguments to an end. The number 3 is the arbitrator, the conciliator, the instrument of harmony and peace. Love, occupation, journeys, friendship, or the expression of your creativity... the omen is excellent whatever your question may be. You do not have force yourself; everything will happen naturally.

3 and the Warrior

Don't doubt your talents and your abilities. The warrior has won the battle. Leave sadness, fear and questioning behind and abandon yourself to your happiness.

3 and the Male

This is a man in your immediate circle whose spirit is very close to yours. This is a friend, a companion on the journey with whom you will share your joys and sorrows.

3 and the Female

This is a woman close to you who appreciates and supplements your talents. If your common projects are undertaken in the spirit of friendship, success is certain.

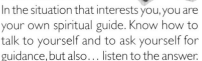

3 and the Chief

In the situation that interests you, you are your own spiritual guide. Know how to talk to yourself and to ask yourself for guidance, but also... listen to the answer.

3 and Cattle

This concerns financial gains resulting from your creative work, from the expression of your artistic or other talents. Investments made now will increase in value over time.

4 • Kune

in Zulu, kune means "he who holds strongly together." Now is the time to stabilize your situation, to unite the various portions of your life and to work with other people on the development of common projects. Don't seek to make progress on your own but see what you can do for others or in agreement with them. Taking pleasure in a job well done, or from carrying out a task or a duty, will always lead to good results. You are not on earth to make only yourself happy but to learn to appreciate what you are doing and to cooperate with others.

4 and the Warrior

Value your happiness. The rewards gained from the efforts that you have made will be greater than you could have hoped for.

4 and the Male

This is a man you can count on. Honest and conscientious, he has the ability to work with others. Don't try to dominate him; deal with him as an equal.

4 and the Female

This is a woman worthy of your respect. If you take your own feelings into account and know how to express the respect that you have for her, nothing can stop you.

4 and the Chief

Everything is possible, and everything is permitted, provided you live in harmony with yourself. Unite your body and spirit, your thoughts and your actions in pursuit of your goal.

4 and Cattle

Your financial affairs or your material problems will soon be resolved. Don't try to accumulate goods. If you let others profit from your possessions, everything will go well.

5 Kuhlanu

According to Zulu tradition, the number 5 symbolizes the imperfection of man. You need to pay great attention and not start anything in an impulsive manner. It is not reason but your emotions and your desires that are leading you. If you are not very careful, problems will follow. What you have accumulated could easily disappear due to an instant of folly or a thoughtless decision. It matters little that what you think of the current situation; nothing should be undertaken. It is necessary to wait, above all calming your heart and your spirit.

5 and the Warrior

You have been engaged in negative or destructive actions, and your are facing a period of instability. You must govern your emotions, not let yourself be led by them. After the tempest, calm will return.

5 and the Male

This is a man with whom you must keep at a distance, at least temporarily. Reconsider your relationship with him. For the moment, emotions are running too high.

5 and the Female

This is a woman with whom you must be very careful. If emotion takes the upper hand, things will turn out badly.

5 and the Chief

In relation to the area that interests you, you must question yourself seriously because you have made some mistakes, you have had negative thoughts, or you have acted too impulsively.

5 and Cattle

Appearances are misleading, and you must be very careful so far as money and material goods are concerned. Weigh up every aspect of the problem, every decision, and do not commit yourself lightly. Otherwise, a loss will follow.

6 ● Isitupa

Symbolized by the lion, the number 6 expresses strength and courage. What you have started earlier, the efforts that you have made, the feelings that you have experienced… all these things must now find fulfillment. Don't put off anything until later. Set priorities and objectives. Face challenges; you will use your strength to overcome them. Roar like a lion, but don't impose your will on others. Help those who need it, those who do not have the same power. You know what is good and what is good for you. Go forward with determination, boldness, and frankness. Don't be afraid of danger.

6 and the Warrior
You have been chosen to carry out an important task. You know what to do, where to go, and whom you are addressing. You have enough strength and determination to bring your projects to a successful conclusion.

6 and the Male
This is a man of great courage, endowed with a strong character, who is a reliable ally for you. As long as you work together, success is certain.

6 and the Female
This is a woman with a strong, honest character. Before engaging in a closer relationship with her, ask yourself what your actual intentions and limitations are. You will then be amazed how this person can help you.

6 and the Chief
Do not be afraid of adversity. You are protected and guided in your actions. Disregard the doubts, hurdles and limits that you have imposed on yourself. You have the necessary strength for the realization of your project.

6 and Cattle
Your initiatives will lead you to success, particularly if it is a matter of financial gain, investments or material goods. Grasp the opportunity that presents itself. This chance may not come again.

7 Isikombisa

The number 7 is considered the "foolish" number, the one that wants to construct situations that seem doomed to failure. In your situation, you must not be afraid of other people. Let them speak and follow their own way. The only important thing is what you yourself must find. This oracle underlines the futility of your efforts, if they are only concerned with the material domain. If you want to make progress, set out to develop on a spiritual plane. Be very careful in the relationships you are engaged in. If you are seeking to imitate others, you will fail straightaway.

7 and the Warrior

You are going in the wrong direction. Revise your objectives, study them from a long-term perspective. Be aware that, when you want to raise yourself up, there is also the risk of failure. Study your past experience and learn its lessons for the future.

7 and the Male

This is a man of your acquaintance who is able to help, but who is waiting for you to be ready to receive assistance and to follow his guidance.

7 and the Female

This is a woman who is ready to help you, so long as the relationships that you are maintaining with her are clear and decisive, and that the questions you ask her are frank and direct.

7 and the Chief

Before putting your question to the oracle, you must first have put it clearly to yourself! But yes, you know all the answers to your questions!

7 and Cattle

This is a question of material benefits, but you must look at the situation more closely. There is something futile or ephemeral in your projects, something pointless…

8 Itoba Minwe Mibili

The symbol of the number 8 is associated with conflict, struggle, and war. It relates to a period of abstinence, privation, or the loss that follows gentler and more prosperous moments. The challenge of the number 8 requires engagement in a struggle that obliges you to live with less comfort and fewer resources. But in the end, you will emerge into a stage of material or spiritual expansion. Remember that nothing is ever gained without loss, and that to receive it is necessary first of all to give. What is new and good will arrive only when you put an idea, a project or an individual to one side, possibly for good.

8 and the Warrior
You have suffered, or are suffering again, from a loss that may be material or psychological. But the warrior entering combat prefers that his adversary be strong. Because of that, the victory is greater.

8 and the Male
This is a man of your acquaintance who is experiencing serious problems and needs your guidance and assistance. Don't turn your back on him; your destiny is linked with his.

8 and the Female
This is a woman who needs you, your presence, your words and who, in return, will help you. Perhaps you will be called to fight alongside of her? If that is the case, be ready to do so. It is in this way that you will preserve your good relationship.

8 and the Chief
In the situation that interests you, you must act with the other person—or other people—in a spirit of justice. Egoism will lead to defeat.

8 and Cattle
Concerning material goods or money, you must fight to keep what you possess and perhaps even yield some ground. It is by sacrificing a little that you will gain much.

9 Itoba Munwa Munye

The number 9 is considered to be a very good omen. It is the symbol of creation, fertility, maternity, the woman, and the child. You are going to enter a period of new ideas, new needs. This is the point of departure, the commencement of a project, and the omen is excellent for everything that involves travel, friendship, a marriage, a meeting, a union, or a cooperation between partners. You must be at the same time strong and flexible, firm and mild in the relationships you have with others. What you plant now has only to germinate and flower in order to give forth its fruits.

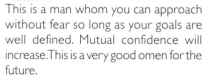

9 and the Male

This is a man whom you can approach without fear so long as your goals are well defined. Mutual confidence will increase. This is a very good omen for the future.

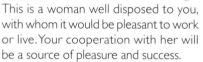

9 and the Female

This is a woman well disposed to you, with whom it would be pleasant to work or live. Your cooperation with her will be a source of pleasure and success.

9 and the Chief

You are not alone. People who are near you are ready to help you, to share your pleasure and your pain. You are in harmony with yourself and, consequently, with the world that surrounds you.

9 and the Warrior

You are blessed by the gods because you are in harmony with the universe. Your wishes will be granted, and your hopes will be crowned with success. It is time for a new way of life and beneficial changes.

9 and Cattle

The period is promising so far as acquisitions, financial gain, and investments are concerned. Efforts initiated now will find their reward.

10 ●Ishumi

The number 10 is considered to be a sacred number because it contains all the qualities of the nine preceding numbers. It symbolizes perfection, achievement, and the final stage of a development. It symbolizes energy and great power over beings and things for those who are sincere in their motivations and persevering in their efforts. The number 10 is the star that guides human beings on the road to their destiny. It is a particularly powerful number, if your question relates to religion, faith, or spirituality.

10 and the Warrior

Do not attach yourself to what is material, earthbound. Shrug off petty or egotistical thinking. Your spirit must be open, free of all jealousy, rancor, and regret. The universe will protect you as long as you live in harmony with yourself.

10 and the Male

This is a man who serves as your guide, master, or professor. You have much to learn from him, but he can learn from you. You complement each other. This is very favorable.

10 and the Female

This is a woman of your circle whom you should get to know better. You are in sync with each other. Your spirits will be joined, and the result will be happiness.

10 and the Chief

You must develop spiritually, and there are one or more people there to help you. The period that is opening up is important, a time of inspiration and of love.

10 and Cattle

When number 10, the spiritual number, coincides with Cattle, symbol of material goods, it means that it is in your spirit, not in your pocketbook, that true richness is situated.

11 Ishumi Na Nye

In the Zulu universe, the number 11 is seen as the number of evil, of demons and of sorcerers. It is also the number associated with spiritualism, clairvoyants, psychic mediums, and those who maintain contact with the dead. But the number 11 does not only have a strange, dark side to show us. It can be very positive if you can overcome the desire to receive only for yourself, and you are capable of giving without expecting anything in return. Egoism must be absolutely banished with number 11. Otherwise, your own demons will take over...

11 and the Warrior
You must delegate some of your responsibilities, ask guidance from reliable people, and not go too far for the moment. Get rid of your bad habits and evil thoughts before starting anything new.

11 and the Male
This is a man with whom you must be very careful because at this moment his presence is not very favorable, your rela-

tionship is unclear, and you will prevent each other from making progress.

11 and the Female
This is a woman with whom a friendly or romantic relationship should be reassessed. You must clarify the situation and understand your own motives. In this way you will understand hers.

11 and the Chief
The problems that you are facing are not due to other people, the overall situation or the environment. You are responsible for them!

11 and Cattle
Look at possible flaws in your current attitude towards money or material possessions. It is up to you to find the solution to your problems.

12 Ishumi Na Mbili

The number 12 is associated with fertility and abundance. It evokes the image of a plant that grows and develops. It is a very beneficial omen, a harbinger of progress in all human activities. The situation in which you find yourself will not remain as it is for long. It will develop, increase, and bloom provided your attitude is completely free from egotistical thinking and that you assume all your responsibilities, both towards other people and towards yourself.

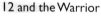

12 and the Warrior

The moment has come to act, not for yourself but for the common good. If you remain positive and if you want to share the benefits of the time, you will enter a period of abundance.

12 and the Male

This is a man of your acquaintance with whom the risks to be taken will bring you greater well-being, provided that you are conscientious in meeting your own responsibilities.

12 and the Female

This is a woman of your circle with whom your relationship will provide good results. Your intentions must remain pure. In this way you will harvest the benefits of this association.

12 and the Chief

Symbol of fertility and abundance, the number 12 indicates success in your enterprises as long as you think more of others than yourself.

12 and Cattle

Your material situation is going to progress, and you will harvest the fruits of your efforts. But you have to help others and share your good fortune.

13 ● Ishamu Na Ntatu

The number 13 is the combination of the unity of the number 1 with the harmony of the number 3. The beneficial effects of 13 are not seen immediately because they develop for a long time in the shadows before becoming manifested. The results are usually unexpected. Consequently the impact of 13 is hard to foresee. The conditions necessary for true harmony in life are present, but for the moment they remain hidden from your eyes. When you least expect it they will emerge from the dark and rise to the surface.

13 and the Warrior
You are capable of creating what you need to live well. But remember: what you want and what you need are not necessarily the same things…

13 and the Male
Professional collaboration, sentimental harmony or disinterested friendship… This involves a man with whom your relationship is strong and will lead to good results.

13 and the Female
This is a woman with whom relations will be constructive and fruitful, as much on the spiritual and material planes as the emotional one.

13 and the Chief
This is a matter of a situation that develops positively in an unexpected way, or of a person you have not seen or thought about for a long time. You may receive news that is as good as it is unlooked for.

13 and Cattle
Hidden forces are working for your material well-being. This means that what you receive may not be exactly what you expected but, with time, it will seem all the more precious to you.

Nordic runes

There are 24 runes in the Futhark, the alphabet used by the ancient Germans, Scandinavians, and Anglo-Saxons, on the basis of which a philosophical and magical system was established. They are used as a mnemonic method by the "master of runes," who orally transmits his knowledge to his disciples. He also uses them also to call upon the gods, to invoke a curse, and to predict the future. The Church prohibited their use in the seventeenth century; however, the practice of divination with runes continued until the industrial revolution in some parts of Great Britain.

Using the Furthark,
the runic alphabet

Carve or mark the 24 runes on stones or pieces of wood, and add an extra unmarked stone or a piece of wood. Put them in a bag and pull out a rune at random to obtain a response.

Alternatively use the wheel opposite to pick a rune as follows.

1

Ask a question about love and relationships. Alternatively, you may put no particular question, in which case the oracle will tell you what awaits you on the emotional plane in the near future.

2

Put your finger on a rune at random.

3

Choose a number between 10 and 25 and count the runes clockwise or counterclockwise as you wish. The rune found in this way determines the oracle.

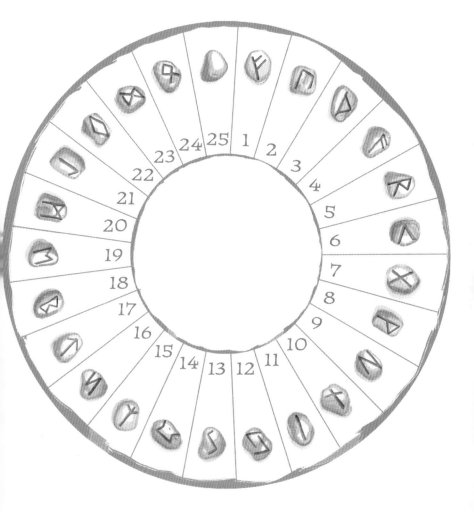

Interpretations

1 • Feoh
CATTLE

Feoh symbolizes cattle, material goods, what one owns and what one makes productive. In love, you must preserve the advantage, stabilize the situation, and maintain your relationship. Now is not the time to start a relationship. If it is a matter of an amorous conquest, act with care and perseverance and in time you will be successful. For the moment, be aware of the luck that you already have.

2 • Ur
AUROCHS

The aurochs or wild buffalo indicates progress, development, the chance of expressing yourself and showing what you are capable of. In love, a natural, beneficial change is taking place. Ur denotes the male sexual impulse and, therefore, passion seems stronger on the part of the man.

3 • Thorn
THE THORN

This indicates a favorable or unexpected change! Here it is a matter of the right person being in the right place at the right time. This rune is a symbol of protection and benevolence. A piece of good news comes from afar. Someone is thinking of you, someone is ready to follow you, to move closer, and to help you. For the moment, do not start anything on your own initiative and, if you lack self-confidence, take no action. A combination of circumstances will be favorable to you.

4 • Ansur
THE MOUTH

This rune, which is more to do with the domain of the spirit than that of the heart or the wallet, speaks of knowledge, education, and training. It is a matter of a test, a trial, a probationary period. In love, you are ingenuous, naïve, a little like an adolescent, and you need a more capable or more experienced person than yourself to give honest and disinterested advice. Do not take any further action; for the moment, talk, communicate, and exchange opinions.

5 • Rad

THE WHEEL

This rune involves journeys, travel, movement, and restlessness. Beware of indecision, so as not to mislead another person or yourself. In love, it is a matter of coming to an understanding with your partner, an exciting, if unconventional, project, a double life or a double language. Keep straight on but don't become complacent. Be ready to make a U-turn, to change your view of the other person, or to discover something or someone else.

7 • Geofu

THE GIFT

This rune involves exchanges, peace, and generosity, with particular relevance to the social and, of course, the romantic domains. Meeting, contact, sharing, marriage… you are on a journey of union. This rune serves as a warning against laziness and hesitation. It involves a gift, a kiss, a beautiful love story that is just beginning. In a couple there is a unity of action and intention. You are at one with your partner: bravo!

6 • Ken
THE FLAME

A positive rune that speaks of a new romantic adventure, of sex, and action. Be optimistic, it is a matter of beginning or beginning again. In love, a meeting is in the air. Sensuality, the fire of passion and warmth, will grow significantly. In a couple, the man is the guide, the one who carries the flame and releases his positive energy. Rely on him.

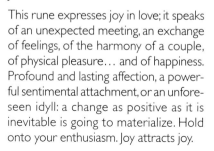

8 • Wynn
JOY

This rune expresses joy in love; it speaks of an unexpected meeting, an exchange of feelings, of the harmony of a couple, of physical pleasure… and of happiness. Profound and lasting affection, a powerful sentimental attachment, or an unforeseen idyll: a change as positive as it is inevitable is going to materialize. Hold onto your enthusiasm. Joy attracts joy.

9 • Hagall
HAIL

The hail that falls suddenly from the sky expresses the hazards of life, the limits imposed, and the pleasant, or unpleasant, surprises that existence reserves for us. You are going to find yourself facing an unexpected event, a surprise or a shock, an interruption or a break. A decision must be taken in response to circumstances beyond your control.

11 • Is
ICE

Don't be impatient if you have to put your plans on hold for the moment. Here it is a matter of lessening momentum, interest, or enthusiasm, a lack of ardor, passion, warmth or sincerity in your relationship; or again, one partner is not free or is afraid of openly expressing emotions. Wait for the situation to improve by itself. Then, but only then, you can act.

10 • Nied
TIME

This rune expresses patience, prudence, and endurance. In short, it symbolizes time, the absolute master. In the situation that concerns or worries you, do not be impatient, greedy, or brutal. In love, the omen is ambivalent or even somewhat negative. Don't attempt anything now; preserve the status quo. Each thing will happen in its own time. For the moment, choose reflection over action and the world of the spirit over that of the flesh.

12 • Jarà
THE HARVEST

Quite simply, you are going to harvest what you have sown. So everything depends on what you have chosen. In love, if there are grains of conflict, the tempest is not far off; watch for the storm! But if you are on the right path, one of sincerity towards yourself and towards others, you will be rewarded with the satisfaction of your desires, a fair return. In any case, what must be will be.

13 • Yr
THE BOW

This rune speaks of danger or the fact of arming oneself against danger. In any case it is a warning. In matters of love don't be too trusting or too suspicious. You must have discernment and follow a happy medium. The goal that you are seeking is within your reach, but, to achieve it, you must now adapt to events and to differences of character, or change your attitude towards your partner.

14 • Peorth
THE SECRET

Is it a secret that you have not revealed? A second chance? Something that is returning? Or an opportunity that presents itself? On the romantic front, this resembles a throw of the die. You will meet with an unexpected opportunity, probably a passionate sexual relationship, a liaison founded only on physical attraction and consequently destined to extinguish itself unless it is fed.

15 • Eolh
IMPETUS

This rune is very positive. It speaks of a new, auspicious influence on your emotions, of love and friendship, of mutual confidence, of optimism and favorable changes. You have confidence in your partner and in your own feelings, and you can trust your intuition to find the one you are looking for. Eolh predicts new challenges, ones that will bring about beneficial changes.

16 • Sigel
THE SUN

Luck, success, and victory! Sigel symbolizes the creative power of the Sun. This is relaxation after tension, the balance found after a troubled period. In love, this rune predicts a luminous meeting, good fortune, and a powerful infusion of energy. Sexual flowering, sensual pleasure, and the satisfaction of love… One caveat: guard against excess, heat stroke, the flash of love at first sight, and other results of exposure to the sun.

17 • Tir
THE ARROW

There is competition and rivalry in the air! This rune speaks of battle, of victory, of a conquest to be made, either of another person or of yourself. With stimulation and motivation, your enthusiasm is growing. In love, passion and fidelity go hand in hand, physical attraction is real, and a sexual relationship is in the offing. This rune speaks more of a lover than a husband, of a mistress than a wife, of a new liaison rather than a current one.

19 • Eoh
THE HORSE

This rune expresses movement: a journey, change, and renewal. Don't wait for anything or anyone; take the reins quickly in hand. Be ready to change your outlook, your self, or your habits. The horse is a sign of progress, an opening, or a new departure. Do not look behind you; you need to move forward. Don't complain, don't reproach yourself at all, be ready to travel physically or spiritually. In romance you will find something new.

18 • Beorc
BIRCH

This is a good omen for those who want to love each other for a long time and to have many children. This rune evokes fertility and fecundity, the birth of a child or an idea, the growth and development of a feeling, or the beginning of a beautiful love story. The projects conceived now must be put into effect immediately. The way to contentment lies in sweetness, tenderness and attention to the details of everyday life.

20 • Mann
THE HUMAN BEING

This rune shows the interdependence that exists between human beings: the brotherhood and friendship that binds them together. Look at things dispassionately. Remain calm; exercise logic. Be careful not to inflame an already volatile situation. Count on the support of others, have faith, speak, listen, exchange views, and, for the moment, look for companionship and friendship rather than love and its possessiveness.

21 • Lagu
WATER

Lagu represents the woman, the mother, the daughter, the feminine in all its aspects, intuition and imagination. For a man, it is a muse, an inspiration, but one that remains dependent on him. For a woman, it promises fertility, artistic gifts, and the creative sense. In love, Lagu forecasts emotion, hypersensitivity, premonitory dreams, fantasies, or a flow of memories. Let yourself be carried along by your internal impulses. You are in the course of creating something.

22 • Ing
ACCOMPLISHMENT

What a good omen! Symbol of fertility and birth, this figure speaks also of every kind of accomplishment. Something ends and something new begins. After the challenges comes the time of relief, of satisfaction, or even a turning point in your existence. A decisive meeting, marital renewal, conception or birth… you are on the eve of a new adventure.

23 • Daeg
THE DAY

A very positive rune that expresses prosperity and progress. It is the light of dawn after the night, the light at the end of the tunnel. It predicts a change in love. You are going to adopt a more positive attitude, and you will have increased clarity of judgment, the opportunity to improve your relationship, and the chance to make genuine and reciprocal feelings grow. A new dawn is rising over your love life.

24 • Odal
POSSESSION

This rune evokes everything that one can buy and, as you know, love is not for sale… In its domain, Odal displays great possessiveness, a fine physical appetite, with eyes bigger than its stomach. You are going too quickly, you are impatient or jealous, your senses dominate you, you are falling for appearances or, again, you are indulging your baser instincts. In this case, look out for problems.

25 • Wyrd
DESTINY

The white rune expresses the inevitable. Reward or punishment, that which is preordained. Or it may only indicate that the oracle does not want to answer you. At least, not now.

The I Ching

The Book of Changes

A masterpiece of wisdom, "The Book of Changes" is one of the founding texts of the Taoist religion, more than 3,000 years old. Used by the Chinese for divination, it reflects the interaction of Yin and Yang. The I Ching answers your questions by describing the current situation, foreseeing developments, and advising on the conduct to adopt in order to balance the forces and also to follow the Tao, the middle way.

Consulting the oracle

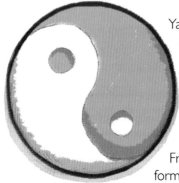

Yang, the active symbol, is represented by an unbroken line:

Yin, the receptive symbol, is represented by a broken line.

From these lines, Yin and Yang, eight trigrams are formed, eight figures each consisting of three lines.

Ch'ien
The father, the creator, the will, the sky

Chen
The elder son, the arouser, difficulty, thunder

K'an
The middle son, the unfathomable, danger, water

Ken
The youngest son, immobility, repose, mountain

K'un
The mother, the receptive, the gift of oneself, the earth

Sun
The elder daughter, sweetness, penetration, wind

Li
The middle daughter, the one who becomes attached, light

Tui
The youngest daughter, joy, stimulation, lake

You will now draw a figure consisting of six lines, a "hexagram," one of the sixty-four figures of the I Ching. It will be the response to your question.

1
Use three identical coins, a pencil, and a sheet of paper.

2
Quiet your mind and think about your question. It must be an important question, one that relates particularly to the heart or to relevant issues. The clearer the question, the better the I Ching's response will be.

3
Throw the three coins at the same time.

4

Add up the value of the three coins. Tails are worth 3; heads are worth 2. The total of the three coins will always be 6, 7, 8 or 9.

5

If the result is 7 or 9, draw a Yang (unbroken) line:

If the result is 6 or 8, draw a Yin (broken) line:

6

Throw the coins five more times to obtain the six lines of the hexagram. Note that you must draw the lines from the bottom to the top, each one above the previous one.

7

Divide what you have drawn into three lower lines and three upper ones, then look them up in the table opposite.

Example

6th line		
5th line		Tui
4th line		
3rd line		
2nd line		Chen
1st line		

This figure is number 17.

Upper Lower	Ch'ien	Chen	K'an	Ken	K'un	Sun	Li	Tui
Ch'ien	1	34	5	26	11	9	14	43
Chen	25	51	3	27	24	42	21	17
K'an	6	40	29	4	7	59	64	47
Ken	33	62	39	52	15	53	56	31
K'un	12	16	8	23	2	20	35	45
Sun	44	32	48	18	46	57	50	28
Li	13	55	63	22	36	37	30	49
Tui	10	54	60	41	19	61	38	58

Interpretations

1 • Ch'ien
STRENGTH

You must be active and creative but at the same time steady in your decisions. Persevere and act, not for yourself but for the common good. For the moment, do not dive into anything. Continue to advance with confidence. You will succeed because you are master of the situation.

3 • Chun
COMMENCEMENT

For the moment, put your ideas in order and think of the steps you have to take. Even if the objective seems remote, don't put things off; you have a great chance of success. There is no action to be carried out immediately; wait for the right moment. Stay confident; you are only at the start, at the very start…

2 • K'un
DEPENDENCE

Show no impatience. Do not act but let yourself be guided; look for support and guidance. Consolidate your position. For the moment, be diplomatic and receptive to any signals that are sent to you. Show sweetness, calm, and perseverance; and you will accomplish your plans.

4 • Mêng
INEXPERIENCE

For the moment, moderate your appetites and discipline yourself. Reflect, forge your character, and do not act out of anger, excitement, or passion. It is necessary to wait for the situation to stabilize itself or materialize before you carry out any plans or launch any action.

5 ● Hsu
WAITING

You must wait. But note, be aware that waiting does not mean simply to hope and do nothing. Rather it means to be certain of achieving the goal. For the moment, relax, increase your self-confidence, and let the situation develop at its own pace. Your enterprise will succeed…in its own time.

7 ● Shih
DISCIPLINE

Do not try to reach your goal by all means possible, do not denigrate anyone, and do not demand from others qualities that you do not have yourself. In your situation, a leader who is able to organize is required, and discipline must be imposed. If you are confident in yourself, take over the management of operations. If not, leave it to other people.

6 ● Sung
CONFLICT

No doubt, the atmosphere is tense. There is a disagreement, a power struggle, but you can control the problem. Don't be too ambitious, understand the origin of the problem, and put yourself a little in the place of the other person. Even if you are right, favor conciliation over conflict. You will benefit from this.

8 ● Pî
UNION

You will not find the answers to your questions along a solitary road. If you want to travel alone, you will not reach your goal. Since conditions are propelling you towards one or several people, go for it! Now is a time for mutual assistance, solidarity, and union.

9 • Hsiao Ch'u
MODERATION

Above all, don't give in to impatience but move forward step by step, accomplishing small things on a daily basis that will produce their effect in the long term. Since events oblige you to pause, learn how to be content with what you have and work on yourself.

11 • T'ai
PROSPERITY

The situation is favorable and that is not by chance! It is thanks to your talents and your qualities that you have succeeded. Carry on in this way but do not rest on the laurels that you do not yet have. Since everything is ready to grow and bloom, take advantage of this period to perfect your actions and express your creativity. You will succeed.

10 Lu
PRECAUTIONS

Do not try to accelerate the pace, overtake others, or achieve your ends at any price. Be careful; one false step and there will be conflict! At this moment you must move forward with caution, on tip-toe. In this way, you will achieve success a little later.

12 P'i
STAGNATION

As circumstances are now unfavorable, you cannot really take action. It is hard for you to communicate, to make yourself understood, and to share. If you try to advance or put yourself forward, you will end up being led astray; and that would be dangerous. For the moment, remain in the shadows, withdraw into yourself, and give yourself time to reflect.

13 • T'ung Jen
TOGETHER

To enjoy the benefits of the union that is in store for you, you must be very honest and sincere, and you must not act in a secretive manner. That would condemn your enterprise to failure. Your interest lies in allying yourself with one person or other people, in order to achieve the benefits together, whether they be material, emotional, or spiritual.

15 • Ch'ien
SIMPLICITY

You will achieve success if you embrace simplicity at all times. For the moment, do not ask too much, do not excite jealousy, do not lie or speak ill of others. Remain in your place and look at your positive and negative qualities with clarity. Increase the one and work on the other, and you will achieve success.

14 Ta Yu
ABUNDANCE

You must rule yourself with a firm will and act with sweetness and benevolence towards those around you. Do not be afraid, have confidence and act with enthusiasm. Then you will overcome all obstacles, even the most difficult.

16 Yu
ENTHUSIASM

Do not give way to discouragement or the negativity of those around you. Free yourself from gray, uninspired thinking, have confidence in yourself, act with optimism, and look at the situation in a positive way. From this infectious enthusiasm success will soon flow!

17 ● Sui
SUPPLENESS

Now is the time to get rid of old problems, resentments, and regrets. Be ready to follow the opportunity of the moment, perhaps even to change your way of life. Be understanding. If you know how to put yourself in the position of someone else or of other people, you will succeed.

19 Lin
EXPANSION

Flushed with the exhilaration of success, don't become careless. From now on, you must be vigilant, because the positive aspects will soon be reversed. You must think about this turnaround of the situation so as to protect yourself against the difficulties to come. Then, you will make yourself master again, and you will succeed.

18 ● Ku
ERRORS

Begin by reflecting on the causes that have led you to this detrimental situation. Then introduce order into your ideas, your feelings, and your life, and decide on another direction. Above all, do not let the situation deteriorate further; respond and all will be well.

20 ● Kuan
STANDING BACK

Stop! Show no excitement or irritation... the situation demands that you calm the flood of your thoughts and reflect calmly. You need clarity before launching an action or making any kind of decision.

21 • Shih Ho
DESTROYING THE OBSTACLE

You must immediately suppress the causes of disagreement and exercise authority to eliminate what is not working. There must be no feebleness, no letting yourself go. Do not let yourself be carried away by discussions but be ready to cut, to judge, and if need be, to punish.

23 Po
DECLINE

Now is not the time to take action or to transform the situation, even if it is unfavorable to you at this moment. Simply be prudent and flexible. At this point, inaction is not cowardice but wisdom.

22 • Pi
SEDUCTION

Don't be impatient; the hour for great actions has not yet struck. Meanwhile, work on harmonizing your relationships. Don't trust appearances; they may turn out to be misleading.

24 • Fu
RENEWAL

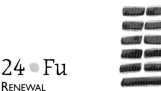

Open your eyes! It is not a matter of precipitating things, otherwise you will waste this renewal that is just dawning. Have no fear, everything will happen at the right time—that is, so long as you do not resort to drastic measures.

25 ● Wu Wang
THE UNEXPECTED

Avoid jealousy, covet nothing, and don't second guess yourself. If you do, you will be heading towards failure. For the moment, do not make hasty decisions. Be sincere, persevering, and ready to put in effort. Then success will come from an unexpected quarter.

26 ● Ta Ch'u
AMBITION

Have confidence. You have considerable assets, particularly for a substantial or long-term project. This is the time to reveal your ambition, to surround yourself with other people and to take action even if, on the face of it, it seems difficult.

27 ● I
TO IMPROVE

Guard against all kinds of excess, in particular too much eating and drinking, and going too fast. Treat your body as a friend, not as a burdensome weight. For the time being, cultivate your character, show proof of your patience and moderation in everything you do and, above all, think before you speak.

28 ● Ta Kuo
EXCESS

Be aware that in the situation you are in, violence or rushing things will achieve nothing. In this exceptional but temporary phase, plan a strategic withdrawal and, even if you must retreat for some time, do not be discouraged. Light will emerge from loneliness!

29 • K'an
DANGER

You must avoid danger and the repetition of danger, and you must show proof of calmness, prudence, and confidence in yourself. Think of the important goals, not of easy, superficial, or short-term matters. Don't be discouraged; if you are sincere, really sincere, you will succeed.

31 • Hsien
ATTRACTION

If you are open, receptive to those around you, and attentive to their problems but also capable of understanding the guidance that is offered to you, then you will achieve success. There is no significant action to follow; simply be ready to join in.

30 • Li
FIRE

Don't think that you are completely independent, don't act in a violent or impulsive manner, and don't let your fire turn in on yourself. For the time being, discipline yourself and take a secondary role. Be determined and don't waste your energy.

32 • Hêng
PERSEVERANCE

You must cultivate steadiness. Keep to your course, thinking not of the short term, but of the future. Look for continuity, loyalty, and patience. Don't take on too much but make progress slowly, in a single direction. Then, you will succeed.

33 ● Tun
RETIREMENT

There is no battle to engage in and no action to take. On the contrary, calm your spirit, find grounds for understanding and, progressively, you will take things in hand. This may seem paradoxical but you will achieve success even if, for the moment, you are not trying to move forward.

34 ● Ta Chuang
ASCENT

This is a very favorable period. You are capable of making your ideas progress and of bringing your undertakings to a satisfactory conclusion. Don't relax your efforts, and don't count on the laurels you have not yet won. Persevere, move ahead, and act without abusing your power. Success is at hand.

35 ● Chin
PROGRESS

In this situation, which is very favorable, move forward with perseverance and equanimity; don't be afraid of anything or anyone. Don't be too ambitious, and don't reproach yourself for not profiting enough from the situation. In this way you will triumph over every obstacle.

36 ● Ming I
DARKNESS

Don't let yourself slip into a spiral of sadness. Don't try to make an impression on others. Conceal your strengths, don't take on too much, and don't look for help. For the moment, leave things as they are. Your strength must be for yourself, not others.

37 • Chia Jên
THE GROUP

At the moment you won't find success in the external world. Stay within your own circle of family, friends, or loved ones. The moment has come to establish sincere relationships and to remain loyal to your commitments. Grand speeches will not be effective; speak with your heart rather than with your mind.

38 • K'uei
OPPOSITION

Above all, don't carry on in a brusque or direct manner because you will create even stronger opposition. For the moment, focus on small improvements, remain calm, and be careful. Distance yourself from those who have nothing to offer you, and become closer to those who can help you effectively.

39 • Chien
THE OBSTACLE

Current circumstances enable you to take stock of the situation. Revise your plans, make a balance sheet or an examination of conscience, and free yourself from what no is longer appropriate for you. Yes, it is wise to stop yourself and perhaps even to take a step backwards. One step back can lead to two steps forward.

40 • Hsieh
DELIVERANCE

Better conditions of life are returning or an obstacle has been removed. It is now necessary to free yourself of the last seeds of conflict, not to linger on the faults you have committed but to finish as quickly as possible so as to make a clear space for something new. This response augurs amity, forgiveness, and reconciliation.

41 ● Sun
MODERATION

Circumstances are difficult at the moment, but don't be bitter, don't be ashamed, and don't envy anyone. For the time being, moderate your lifestyle, reduce your passions and appetites, and return to greater simplicity. In this way you will find the internal strength necessary for your next success.

43 ● Kuai
DETERMINATION

Put an end to confused or dubious situations. Don't compromise with other people or with yourself. You must act with determination; don't hesitate to transform things radically if necessary. Be resolute, even if that means creating friction.

42 ● I
INCREASE

Your situation is good if not excellent! You are in a fortunate, successful phase. The oracle speaks of growth and expansion, and it is responding positively to your question. But look out, you will have to put in some effort to take advantage of this favorable period.

44 ● Kou
TEMPTATION

Don't give in to temptation! Be wary of trying to impress, of false promises, of what seems flashy or fabulous. If a person or a situation initially seems inoffensive, look out. There is a risk that he, she, or it will turn against you or manipulate you. Be very careful.

45 • Ts'ui
GATHERING

To achieve success, it is necessary henceforth to start an action, to accept guidance from reliable people, to establish solid links, and to gather together what is scattered. Also be aware that precautions must be taken because conflicts can easily come into existence.

47 • K'un
ADVERSITY

Weakness, sadness, and regrets must be eliminated immediately. Above all, you must not give in to discouragement. Identify your mistakes so as to correct them, remaining serene in the face of adversity. Meet your commitments, remain loyal to yourself, and think of the future rather than the past.

46 • Shêng
SUCCESS

Yes, success will definitely appear and, to achieve it, it is necessary simply to put yourself to work, to supply the necessary effort. That's it, go forward, look for people who possess power and authority, and show them your talents. This is the sign of a promotion, of an upward trend... bravo!

48 • Ching
ENDEAVOR

To resolve the question that was asked, you must express what you are keeping deep within yourself. Efforts must be made and a personal search into yourself must be undertaken. Establish the rules of a healthy life and follow them. For the moment, don't concern yourself with other people, or another person, but only with yourself.

49 ● Ko
CHANGING

If you understand that change is necessary, then you will overcome every obstacle. You will have recognized that this is natural and you will be master of events because they will no longer scare you. It is the end of something, the beginning of something else, and this heralds great success!

51 ● Chên
THE UNEXPECTED

Faced with emotions that can trouble your mind, you must preserve your judgment and not give in to anxiety, lack of concern or impatience. The situation that interests you has only to begin. For the moment, relax. In this way you will recognize the opportunities that are to come.

50 ● Ting
THE GOOD WAY

This is the time to improve yourself, to perfect yourself, and to keep yourself ready to welcome what is new. Move forward calmly and with determination; pay attention to all events, even minor ones, that may occur. Then you will be ready to achieve great things!

52 ● Kên
STILLNESS

Attention, don't let your thoughts go further than the situation requires. Above all don't try to move forward, or you will find yourself once more at a dead end. It is better to rest your body and your mind, to relax, if only for a few hours. Then, but only then, can you begin to move forward again.

53 ● Chien
DEVELOPMENT

Whether it is a matter of love or work, don't be in a hurry to do well, or you will do badly. Look at things in the long term and let your plan progress through each stage of development. It is a plan that demands patience and steadfastness. You are well aware of that...

55 ● Fêng
RADIANCE

There is nothing to be afraid of; everything will go well! So, enjoy yourself, take advantage of what you already have, and allow others to benefit as well. This response is the sign of great radiance and, without any doubt, you will reach your goals.

54 ● Kuei Mei
AMBIGUITY

You want immediate satisfaction, but that is a mistake. Before associating yourself with others, or another individual, know your opinions and express them clearly. For the moment, don't give in to impulsiveness and don't make decisions out of passion or impatience. In short, be reasonable...

56 ● Lu
INSTABILITY

When you cannot put yourself to the fore, when your position is unstable, you must be careful and reserved and choose your relationships and associates with care. In particular, you must not be insistent or hang idly about. Then, you can continue on your way. It is a journey that will lead, in time, to success.

57 • Sun
MILDNESS

In your situation, don't look for violent methods and don't give in to impatience but act with gentleness, developing your ideas little by little. Take your time, take the long term view, and be determined; then you will overcome every obstacle.

59 • Huan
DISPERSION

You will arrive at a positive result if you think of others as well as yourself. Don't act dramatically, accept things as they are, renew the threads of dialogue, and look for reconciliation.

58 • Tui
JOY

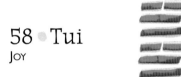

Don't keep what you feel to yourself; share it with others. Yes, joy is infectious and that is why you must continue on the path that you are taking. The exchange of feelings and ideas will result in enrichment for all concerned.

60 • Chieh
LIMITATIONS

Above all, avoid excess and impulsive actions. Be aware that even freedom has its limits. For the moment, decide on a rule of conduct and follow it. Save your strength, discipline yourself, and don't be lax or too severe, either with others or with yourself.

61 • Chung Fu
SINCERITY

You will find yourself facing recalcitrant people who are hard to influence or very different from you. Rid yourself of prejudice and theoretical assumptions. Don't deceive yourself. If you are sincere others will respond, and you will be successful.

62 • Hsiao Kuo
ECONOMY

Be humble, gentle and careful, because, for the moment, you cannot achieve great things. On the other hand, pay attention to details, fill in the gaps, and save your strength, your ideas, and your money. Your future success will depend on these economies.

63 • Chi Chi
BALANCE

This oracle encourages you to reflect on the course of events, to maintain your efforts and, in particular, to remain vigilant. Don't give in to the easy option. You must show strength and firmness, and thus you will hold onto the results you have achieved.

64 • Wei Chi
RESPONSIBILITIES

Do not embark upon bold or precipitous actions. The situation is difficult but may turn out well, as long as you are very careful. Advance step by step and examine the interplay of the people and forces that surround you. Think first, then act.

Numerology

Chaldeans, Egyptians, Hebrews, Chinese, Hindus, Greeks... all of these peoples have used the symbolism of numbers to build temples or to acquire knowledge of sacred things. In the course of the centuries, numbers lost their symbolism in favor of pure mathematics. Then in the early twentieth century, numerology reappeared as a means of studying personality. Three women originally from the west coast of the United States were the source of some simple and effective methods.

Using numerology

In numerology, life is divided into cycles of nine years.

1

To find out what year of the cycle you are in and what you may expect, **add together the month and the day of your birth and the year that you want to study**. (The year of your birth is not taken into account.)

2

Reduce the result to obtain a number between 1 and 9.

Example:

Prediction for the year 2005
for a person born on August 22nd (8/22):

8 + 22 + 2005 = 2035

2035, that is 2 + 0 + 3 + 5 = 10

and 10 is 1 + 0 = 1

In 2005, this person born on August 22nd will be in year 1, the first year of the new cycle.

The symbolism of numbers

4 is stability, the symbol of fulfillment, discipline, work, and construction.

5 is halfway between 1 and 9. It is the free arbiter, the symbol of liberty, mobility, and change.

3 is expansion, the symbol of expressiveness, creativity, communication, and adaptation.

1 is the principle of creation, the symbol of energy, action, and enthusiasm.

9 marks achievement. It is the symbol of the ideal and of altruism, and it is the number of the human dimension.

2 is duality, the symbol of association, independence, and balance or loss of balance.

6 is harmony, the symbol of perfection, balance, and responsibility.

8 is materialism, the symbol of ambition, power, success, and authority.

7 is spirituality, the symbol of reflection, wisdom, and research into truth.

Interpretations

Year 1

Move forward! Don't wallow in the past or regret what might have been; this year puts you on the starting line. Now it is necessary to look far ahead, to launch yourself into a new adventure and, if need be, to return to zero. Or rather, to 1! A new cycle of nine years is getting under way so this is the time to carry out new plans and to have faith in them.

What you should do
In year 1, all that is needed is to begin. Be a little bit egoistic, act for yourself, and enjoy yourself. You will not yet be aware of what is in the process of changing in your life, but you will notice this more in the course the cycle. For the moment, throw yourself into it.

To avoid
Avoid standing still. Don't try to bring a matter to a conclusion, work on what is past, rest on your laurels, or devote yourself to others. Don't worry about the details, just turn on the ignition and step on the gas.

At work
Now is the time to change direction and to commit yourself to a new, unknown course. Do something different, something that is worthwhile, and gamble with the future. Begin an activity, interest yourself in what you do not know, and put your own talents into effect. Don't wait for anyone's help; rely only on yourself.

As a couple
You may feel a little isolated—this is normal in year 1. Don't stay tied to anyone but be independent, follow your own path, stand back or even far away. For you, rebirth is in the air. Warn your partner that you need your freedom.

On your own?
In this year of autonomy, live comfortably with yourself, appreciating and developing your talents. A little later, you will meet the person with whom you will share things.

Year 2

If the past year has brought you to a new environment, if a situation has taken shape, or if a person has appeared, you are now going to cooperate closely. Year 2 is the year of union and disunity. In the event of profound disagreement or opposition, a break-up is likely.

What you should do
This is the period for consolidating an association, or even for marriage. Go towards others, or another person, emerge from your egoism, your solitude, and your shell. Be happy to take part in the world that surrounds you.

To avoid
Impatience and brusqueness. Don't provoke tensions because you can easily come into conflict. Things will move slowly, and you will be dependent on someone else or other people. Since it is the time for discussion, negotiation, and the establishment of common goals, be flexible, perceptive, and diplomatic.

At work
Don't seek to do things on your own. Your are going to go into partnership, sign a contract, work as part of a team, collaborate, and use your strengths in common. But also look out for tensions with your superiors or colleagues and, if need be, the end of a partnership or a cooperation.

As a couple
The number 2 looks both ways. Everything depends on your current situation. If your love was floundering, it will fall to the ground. There may be a temporary or final separation; in this case, it is the other person who will decide it. On the positive side, look for associations, reconciliation, a stimulating sharing of life, and unknown sensual horizons.

On your own?
Now is the time to meet someone! Year 2 announces a connection, hitting it off with someone, goals in common … a couple is forming! Engagement? Marriage? Everything is possible, so open your eyes and your heart.

Year 3

Good news: the number 3 expresses a burst of speed, an acceleration of movement! In your life, situations are going to reach a new level. Everything moves quickly! It is an interesting, volatile period, with many aspects and many encounters.

What you should do

Throw yourself into this year of renewal without preconceived ideas, without ready-made assumptions. Let yourself be carried. Be inquisitive, open, and eager to learn, to know, and to meet others. Move, change, and travel… amuse yourself!

To avoid

Sadness, melancholy, and dullness. Your routine will be shaken up and your living habits will take a knock. Don't try to hold on to your reference points at all costs; on the contrary, you must adapt yourself to this pace and follow the movement, even if you feel rushed.

At work

Don't look for responsibility, promotion, or financial benefits. Spread yourself about a bit. It is the moment to express your talents, to do something else or in another way, to inform yourself, to communicate, and to move about. There is also a leisure or creative activity that you want to do and have not yet started. Now is the time.

As a couple

It is a time of daily renewal. Your life together is enriched by contacts with new acquaintances and new friends. Perhaps there is a move in store, home expansion, or the birth of a child.

On your own?

An auspicious period! Your contacts multiply, there is the discovery of another place, and there are outings, amusements, and travel… your enthusiasm will bring imitators. This year, express yourself, flirt, and vary your pleasures.

Year 4

Now, you have to roll up your sleeves and get down to work! 4 is the square number, fixed and weighty, indicating a period of stabilization. Last year was the time for sampling different experiences and adventures; transformation is still in the future. That will be for the next year. Now it is a matter of maintaining, preserving, and completing what already exists.

What you should do
Dig a solid foundation for your existence, discover, or rediscover, your reference points, stick to what you know and to what you have. Of course, the pace of this year is slow. You will have obligations towards others and towards yourself. Take the helm and move forward slowly and steadily.

To avoid
Impatience and lack of concentration. Don't try to speed things up or rush people or situations, but tie up loose ends, restrict yourself, and economize. There is nothing to change, but everything to organize.

At work
The atmosphere is not pleasant or light. You are asked to come to terms with your responsibilities, and even those of others to yourself, to make great efforts, to accomplish your task, in short… to work. Be serious, disciplined, and determined, and you will move forwards.

As a couple
The situation remains steady, which is not too bad… The year 4, more centered on work than on feelings, above all enables you to establish reliable, solid foundations, from which together you will grow. Fidelity and honesty are essential.

On your own?
Anything can happen, of course, but it must be said that the number 4 does not bode well for meeting new people. Number 5 will be perfect for that. For the time being, learn to wait and be comfortable with yourself. Your patience will be rewarded.

Year 5

You have arrived at the halfway point in the cycle of 9 years, at the very middle of the ford. Year number 5 is a transitional year. In it, things are going to affect you and situations are changing. You are going to renew yourself and break with the past. What cannot last any longer will disappear, while what is new will make its appearance.

What you should do

It is the moment to shake up your routine and throw yourself into the unknown. You are impatient, that is normal, but you are also active, ready to change your direction or destination. Go with it, be confident, follow your impulses, and bet on what is new.

To avoid

Stagnation. Don't organize things too much, let in air, light, and new faces. Don't put the brakes on movement, follow the flow even if it seems fast and dangerous. The only mistake would be missing the opportunities that present themselves.

At work

At the end of the year, will you be doing the same thing as today? Nothing is less likely! Open up the field of the possible: change your direction, your ideas, your specialty, your job, your employer, your route, or your timetable. There is a super-charged atmosphere, a frantic pace, stress is there, yes, but it will motivate you.

As a couple

You will feel independent and consequently anything can happen. If your situation is difficult, you will choose the emergency exit, you will see another side, and you will live your own life. This year, you must renew yourself, either alone or together.

On your own?

This year has been dedicated to you! Many encounters, love at first sight, passion in all its forms, new experiences… don't make too much of them but wait for next year to take a decision or involve yourself completely.

Year 6

In the cycle of 9 years, one year is considered particularly beneficial: year 6. This brings balm to the heart, the spirit, and the bank account; it improves the ordinary and can reveal the extraordinary. Things flow from the source, relationships are created, and harmony prevails. Life seems simple.

What you should do

Give and receive. This year calls for the sense of responsibility, maturity, and generosity. You are going to cross a threshold, grow, and even blossom. Continue to be yourself, love other people, and you will find a meaning to your life.

To avoid

Egoism that makes you miss the chance of being happy. Restlessness that will prevent you from doing important things, from deciding on a direction and taking your life in hand.

At work

Excellent prospects! There is progress, a promotion, an increase in your income, your talents are recognized, and you are an artistic success. The atmosphere is calm, harmonious, and productive. You will have the needed self-confidence. It is up to you to begin; you will be rewarded.

As a couple

This is a fertile period in every sense of the word. You will decide to live together, you will buy a house, you will get married, you will expect a child, or the family will take on a particular importance. This year you will be capable of receiving everything that love has to offer you.

On your own?

Enjoy yourself! The events of the past year will fall into place. The time has come for becoming involved, for meeting someone, for getting engaged or for getting together. Dedicated to love, year 6 reserves its sweet, juicy fruits for you. Indulge yourself!

Year 7

The seven days of creation, and on the seventh day the Lord rested… Year 7 demands detachment, depth, and reflection. It is a year of some isolation, deliberate or involuntary. It puts questions to you, and you do not yet have the answers for decision, action, or achievement. That will be in year 8. The uneven number 7 relates to the mental, intellectual, and spiritual domain. In this area, you are going to mature.

What you should do
The pace is slow or up and down. It is the time to study, to look for things, and to understand. Ask yourself what you want, choose to live your life, and question yourself. There is the possibility of escape, of traveling in body or mind, or of sawing through the bars of your cage.

To avoid
Don't try to earn money, seize power, or cause a particular situation to happen. Also, it is useless to look ahead or make plans; year 7 is one of surprises and the unexpected.

At work
Apart from a sudden transfer, don't expect to make upward progress. Be original, think more about yourself than your work, and don't take any fundamental decisions. Escape from it and take a sabbatical year.

As a couple
You are going to ask yourself some questions, perhaps about someone else, and certainly about yourself. What is the quality of your love and your ties? If you are in doubt, you will bring about a temporary break; if there is a major problem, the break will be final.

On your own?
In year 7 the correct way must be followed, so this year celibacy will be good for you. But look out, not everything is determined. There is something unexpected in the air…

Year 8

This is the year of achievement. What you have sown in previous years will now finds its reward—or its punishment, it all depends on what you have sown… So this will be a peak, the recognition of your work, the fruit of your efforts, and a just return for what you have done. Alternatively, if you have been improvident, unjust or lazy, it will be a painful time.

What you should do

Take things in hand, make a decision, sign up, accept or refuse, but don't dither. This year requires you to take on all your responsibilities, to advance, to develop, to engage yourself, and to make a choice. Now your thoughts and actions are going to become a reality.

To avoid

Absenteeism, letting things go, idleness, illusions, hesitation, loss of self-confidence, and fear of growing up.

At work

Depending upon your current situation, year 8 will bring an excellent promotion, material success, the achievement of something substantial, or financial gains; or, in the case of improvidence, it indicates loss, failure, or penalties. You have the controls in your hand, and you are in possession of the power to act on events. Use it.

As a couple

You make things official, you say "yes," you live together, you decide to have a child, you buy an apartment or a house, you invest, and you have a lot of emotion invested. But feelings are powerful, so watch out for jealousy! In the event of an actual problem, there will be a break-up and this time you're the one who will decide on it.

On your own?

What you have previously overcome will not have been in vain! There may be a meeting, a decisive choice, a long negotiation successfully concluded, ties that were not apparent but have now become so, or else there is the exhilaration of the senses and fiery passions.

Year 9

The final year of your cycle. But before beginning another year, you must free yourself from excess, from what no longer suits you, slows you down, irritates you or exhausts you. This cleansing will completely restore you once more and in the month of October you will set off again on a new nine-year cycle!

What you should do
First, rid yourself of ideas that are no longer current, objects that weigh you down, situations that complicate your existence, and people who bring you nothing. With whom and with what, are you going to begin again?

To avoid
Materialism, hunger for power, violence, and egoism. Take the heat out of the debate and look at your situation from higher up, from further away.

At work
This is the moment to extricate yourself from a position in which you feel trapped, to put an end to the arrangement, to hand in your resignation, to sell this house or that business, to take retirement, to separate yourself from responsibilities, to relax the pressure, and to get out of your rut.

As a couple
If things are going well, look forward to the culmination of your relationship, a better knowledge of the other person, or the discovery of a new understanding. If your situation is difficult, there is a temporary remoteness; if it is very difficult, there will be a break-up and, in this case, the other person will decide on it.

On your own?
Year 9 speaks more of friendly ties than sentimental ones. This is the moment to cultivate friendship, to travel, and to discover other ways of life. Be open and generous, feel free but do not start anything important before the month of October. For the time being, bring things to a conclusion.

Jogo dos buzios

Brazilian divination

Originally borrowed from the Yoruba people of Nigeria, this divinatory game using cowrie shells was brought to Brazil by the slaves in the sixteenth and seventeenth centuries—hence its name Jogo dos buzios, "the game of the cowries." The shells answer your questions through the intermediary of the Orixas, the gods of the Santeria Afro-Brazilian religion. Cowries have a smooth side, known as "closed," and a side with a narrow opening, known as "open." They can be replaced by other small shells found on beaches.

How to go about it

1

Find sixteen shells or coffee beans.

2

Find a place where you will be quiet, with a sandy or beaten earth surface or even a wooden surface such as a table. If possible, have someone beat a drum.

3

Draw a circle on the ground to mark the boundary of the space devoted to the game of divination. If working on a table, draw an imaginary circle.

4

Ask the questioner to listen to the drum with eyes closed, then when it falls silent, to concentrate on the question.

5

Take the sixteen shells or coffee beans in your hands, bring them close to your forehead, then throw them on the ground or table.

6

Count the shells that show their open side. If you are using coffee beans, count the slit sides.

7

Read the interpretation and guidance of the symbol indicated by the number of open shells.

The Orixas

Oxala

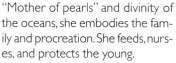

Father of the Orixas, he is the beginning and the end. He symbolizes peace and equilibrium.

Oxum

Goddess of the rivers and clear, fresh waters, she embodies beauty, sensuality, and artistic talent. Feminine and receptive, she is also capricious and jealous.

Exu

Sentry, guardian, and mankind's ambassador to the Orixas, he is the tempter. As wild as he is creative, he destroys and transforms in order to rebuild.

Ogun

The god of warriors and hunters, he symbolizes courage, strength, and truth. Depending on the draw, he is the liberator or executioner.

Yemanja

"Mother of pearls" and divinity of the oceans, she embodies the family and procreation. She feeds, nurses, and protects the young.

Xango

At the sound of drums and music, Xango is thunder and lightning. A virile protector, he embodies authority, willpower, and domination.

Oxossi

A two-faced god, one face positive and dynamic, and the other artistic, dreamy, and passive.

Nana

Rain goddess and guardian of the Underworld, Nana is the grandmother. She embodies calm and level-headedness.

The Ibejis

The cosmic twins represent play, freedom from care, and the innocence of childhood.

Note: the letter "x" is pronounced "sh."

Interpretations

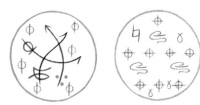

1 open: Okaran
SUCCESS

Exu speaks: "You have a lot of trump cards, you want to take action; you are ambitious." To your question, the answer is "yes," you will succeed and overcome the obstacles, but on the condition that you face up to truth and reality, stand back, and reassess the situation. Indeed, your powerful ego is blinding you. It is by overcoming your desire to take action that you will soon achieve success.

2 open: Okeyu
TRIUMPH

Oxala and the Ibejis speak: "Success, happiness, an end to problems or suffering, you will obtain what you are looking for." This very positive figure combines the freshness of the Ibejis with the wisdom of Oxala and heralds a meeting, a sentimental union, a lucrative job, triumph over enemies, the end of conflict, or simply news that will bring you great joy.

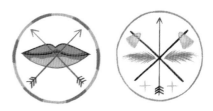

3 open: Ogunda
THE OBSTACLE

Ogun speaks: "You are thinking of an important project, but you are running into difficulties." You will succeed but only if you act honestly, controlling your urges and your strengths. An obstacle must be overcome or even destroyed. You need courage and perseverance as well as self-control. Then, there is no doubt that your efforts will be rewarded.

4 open: Irosun
THE DREAM

Oxossi and Xango speak: "You are determined and proud, even domineering or arrogant, but doubt, indecision, laziness or dreaming are blurring reality." You believe in it without really believing in it. You would like this… you hope that… but if you do nothing to achieve it, you must expect obstacles, problems even impossibilities.

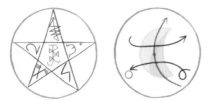

5 open: Oxe
FERTILITY

Oxum and Yemanja speak: "You are pro-tected, which heralds the end of your problems, great success, riches, an encounter, a union, and fertility." Be ambi-tious, have faith in yourself, seize any opportunity that presents itself and, most importantly, take action. Otherwise you risk losing everything. If you hope to win, you will win; your hopes will come true.

6 open: Obara
HESITATION

Xango and Exu speak: "You are trying to change things, perhaps even destroy them in order to rebuild, using your willpower, hard work, feelings or creativ-ity, but you do not know where to begin…" For the moment, look for help, guidance, and support but do not miss any opportunity; it will be worth it. In love you will benefit from help from an unex-pected quarter. Any problems you expe-rience will be short-lived.

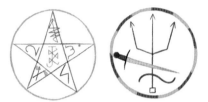

7 open: Odi
ANXIETY

8 open: Ogbe
IMPULSIVENESS

Oxum and Ogun speak: "You love pleasure, riches, and an easy life, and you are ambitious." Yet, you are worried about the future, torn between the desire to act and to let things be, between the desire to change and to stabilize. In love, you will fail if you do not know how to behave; in other fields you need to have faith. You have strengths, but you need to learn how to direct them.

Xango speaks: "You are protected on a spiritual level but guard against aggressiveness, passion or the desire to dominate." Yes, you are impulsive, you want a lot. Be careful, don't be guided by impatience or act on a whim; you would miss many good things that are promised to you. For the moment, calm your mind. Your time will come.

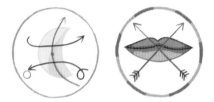

9 open: Osa
PROTECTION

Yemanja and Oxossi speak: "You have great strengths, but you must learn to identify them and nourish them in order to progress." Learn to hold your tongue and take care of yourself. You are protected; everything will be all right so long as you motivate yourself and do not choose the easy option or give in to criticism. You are entirely responsible for your actions.

10 open: Ofun
SEDUCTION

Oxum speaks: "Union, association, charm, seduction, a love affair… you are fascinated by magic, you are carried away by your feelings, and you are guided by your sensuality…" Ofun involves art or the beauty of a person. Be sincere towards yourself and honest with the other person. Don't follow your urges blindly. Remain level-headed and do not enter into a union if your intuition tells you that it will not work. If necessary, ask for advice, and you will receive it.

11 open: Oworin
MYSTERY

12 open: Otupuron
PRIDE

Exu speaks: "Obscure desires, temptation, sexuality, mystery, chaos... the situation is a difficult, complicated one and
it troubles you." It is important to fight
back, to get rid of counterproductive
feelings and thoughts in order to start
on a new footing. This is possible as long
as you find within yourself a balance
between positive and negative forces,
because you are capable of expressing
both equally well.

Xango speaks: "Initiative, decision-mak-
ing, pride, and arrogance... the situation
requires that you show some self-
restraint, respect the law or laws, and do
not try to dominate anyone." In the case
of a problem with the opposite sex,
everything depends on what you say. If
your words are knives they might cut
your own lips! Turn your tongue seven
times in your mouth before saying anything more.

13   open: Ika
WISDOM

14 open: Iwori
HOPE

Nana speaks:"Here it is more a matter of wisdom than of passion, more of honest work than of easy gains." On the romantic front, you must first love before making someone love you. You have reached the end of a cycle, of a story, of an idea, of a thought. This heralds the beginning of something else. But before that you must understand that everything is born, lives, and then dies. Calm, patience, level-headedness, comprehension, and self-control are your trump cards.

Nana, Oxum, and the Ibejis speak:"Happiness in love, prosperity in business, joy in friendship!" This is good news; you find an effective strategy, and there are pleasures to be enjoyed. Now is a time for hope. You are going to be agreeably surprised. This is a culmination, a reward, an awakening, a new event. You have freshness in your feelings as well as charm and self-confidence. You will go far and these good feelings will last a long time!

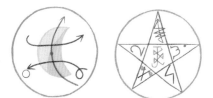

15 open: Otura
ADVERSITY

Yemanja and Oxum speak: "You are constantly asking yourself questions, success is eluding you, you are experiencing adversity, you are subject to bad influences, or perhaps you are dreaming of an impossible love…" In this situation you must be rigorous, patient, true to yourself, and sincere at all times. Make an effort to improve yourself and remember the saying: "Truth is like gold. Keep it inside yourself, and, in the end, you will discover it is still intact."

16 open: Irete
LIGHT

All the Orixas speak: "Your difficulties are behind you now; problems have been solved, so do not worry any more. Now the Sun is shining and illuminating everything around, and truth is triumphant." This figure speaks of financial gain, a successful trip, recovery, serenity, interesting proposals, love with a happy outcome, and lasting happiness. Share this light and be generous.

16 closed: Opira
SILENCE

The Orixas refuse to speak. This figure cancels the game. You must throw the shells again but not today… leave it until tomorrow.

Mahabo

Burmese divination

In the eleventh century, when Anawratha, king of Burma, declared Buddhism the nation's official religion, the monks were the guardians of the esoteric sciences. Later these bonzes concentrated on sacred texts and left the task of predicting the future to astrologers and soothsayers. Today the thousands of pagodas that are scattered across Burma are places of worship and meditation, and it is there that the hu ja, the "soothsayers," practice the art of divination. "Horary divination" is one of the numerous methods used by Burmese soothsayers. It is based on the day of the week on which the questioner was born (Monday, Tuesday, etc.), and the time and day of the week when the question is asked.

What day of the week were you born on?

1

Look up the **year of your birth** in the table opposite and continue along the same line until you reach the column of the **month of your birth**. Write down the number where the two cross: it is the number A.

2

Add to it the **date of your birth**:
number A + date of birth = number B

3

Look up number B in the table below to find the day of the week on which you were born.

Example

1 For a person born on April 23rd, 1957, look for "1957" on the table opposite and continue until you reach the "April" column. Note the number that you find there, **1**.

2 Add this number 1 to the date of birth, "23," that is, 1 + 23 = **24**.

3 Look for "24" in the table below and you will find that the person was born on a "**Tuesday**."

1	8	15	22	29	36	Sunday
2	9	16	23	30	37	Monday
3	10	17	24	31		Tuesday
4	11	18	25	32		Wednesday
5	12	19	26	33		Thursday
6	13	20	27	34		Friday
7	14	21	28	35		Saturday

Years				Jan.	Féb.	Mar.	Apr.	Mar.	Jun.	Jul.	Aug.	Sep.	Oct.	Nov.	Dec.
	1925	1953	1981	4	0	0	3	5	1	3	6	2	4	0	2
	1926	1954	1982	5	1	1	4	6	2	4	0	3	5	1	3
	1927	1955	1983	6	2	2	5	0	3	5	1	4	6	2	4
	1928	1956	1984	0	3	4	0	2	5	0	3	6	1	4	6
1901	1929	1957	1985	2	5	5	1	3	6	1	4	0	2	5	0
1902	1930	1958	1986	3	6	6	2	4	0	2	5	1	3	6	1
1903	1931	1959	1987	4	0	0	3	5	1	3	6	2	4	0	2
1904	1932	1960	1988	5	1	2	5	0	3	5	1	4	6	2	4
1905	1933	1961	1989	0	3	3	6	1	4	6	2	5	0	3	5
1906	1934	1962	1990	1	4	4	0	2	5	0	3	6	1	4	6
1907	1935	1963	1991	2	5	5	1	3	6	1	4	0	2	5	0
1908	1936	1964	1992	3	6	0	3	5	1	3	6	2	4	0	2
1909	1937	1965	1993	5	1	1	4	6	2	4	0	3	5	1	3
1910	1938	1966	1994	6	2	2	5	0	3	5	1	4	6	2	4
1911	1939	1967	1995	0	3	3	6	1	4	6	2	5	0	3	5
1912	1940	1968	1996	1	4	5	1	3	6	1	4	0	2	5	0
1913	1941	1969	1997	3	6	6	2	4	0	2	5	1	3	6	1
1914	1942	1970	1998	4	0	0	3	5	1	3	6	2	4	0	2
1915	1943	1971	1999	5	1	1	4	6	2	4	0	3	5	1	3
1916	1944	1972	2000	6	2	3	6	1	4	6	2	5	0	3	5
1917	1945	1973	2001	1	4	4	0	2	5	0	3	6	1	4	6
1918	1946	1974	2002	2	5	5	1	3	6	1	4	0	2	5	0
1919	1947	1975	2003	3	6	6	2	4	0	2	5	1	3	6	1
1920	1948	1976	2004	4	0	1	4	6	2	4	0	3	5	1	3
1921	1949	1977	2005	6	2	2	5	0	3	5	1	4	6	2	4
1922	1950	1978	2006	0	3	3	6	1	4	6	2	5	0	3	5
1923	1951	1979	2007	1	4	4	0	2	5	0	3	6	1	4	6
1924	1952	1980	2008	2	5	6	2	4	0	2	5	1	3	6	1

How to go about it

1

Ask the question orally or in written form.

2

Note the day of the week and the time that you asked the question.

3

In the table below, look for the row that corresponds to the day of the week and the column corresponding to the time at which you asked the question. You will find a number at the point where the row and column intersect. This is the number of the symbol that concerns you.

4

Look up this symbol in the following pages and read the oracle according to the day of the week of your birth, which you will have established by following the method explained in the previous pages.

	6–8 22–23	8–10 23–0	10–12 0–1	12–14 1–2	14–16 2–3	16–18 3–4	18–20 4–5	20–22 5–6
Sunday	1	6	4	2	7	5	3	1
Monday	2	7	5	3	1	6	4	2
Tuesday	3	1	6	4	2	7	5	3
Wednesday	4	2	7	5	3	1	6	4
Thursday	5	3	1	6	4	2	7	5
Friday	6	4	2	7	5	3	1	6
Saturday	7	5	3	1	6	4	2	7

Example

1 Born on a Wednesday, you are asking the question on a Monday at 12:45 P.M.

2 In the table at the bottom of the opposite page, look at the row for "Monday" and the column that includes 12:45 P.M., that is, "12:00–2:00 P.M." At the intersection of this row and column, you will find the number 3.

3 Look up the symbol 3, Saturn, on page 226. The paragraph for "Wednesday" is the reply to your question.

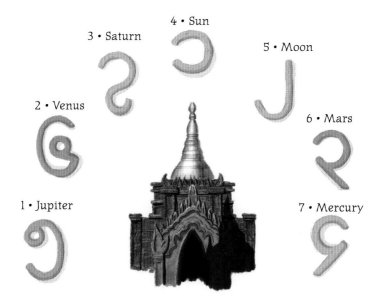

4 • Sun

3 • Saturn

5 • Moon

2 • Venus

6 • Mars

1 • Jupiter

7 • Mercury

In Burma, as in the West, the days of the week fall under the influence of the planets: the Moon (Monday), Mars (Tuesday), Mercury (Wednesday), Jupiter or Thor (Thursday), Venus or Freya (Friday), and Saturn (Saturday); finally, Sunday is the day of the Sun.

Interpretations

1 Jupiter

Born on a Sunday

You are torn between opposing thoughts, your heart is wavering, and you are hesitating. Nonetheless, the omen is good and promises success, especially if your question is related to love or involves traveling. The time has come to make a clear, definite decision and to act with determination. But be careful: this decision must not hurt anyone. Make sure that your objective is disinterested and noble.

Born on a Monday

The omen is excellent. You will be helped by a woman. Learn to listen and act according to your intuition. It will lead you to success.

Born on a Tuesday

This symbol is not favorable for you. There are misunderstandings and problems, and you cannot act immediately. A job has not been completed, and your relationship still lacks harmony. Yet in the medium term, influences will change and become positive. Wait for the right time to act or take a decision. Perseverance will lead to success.

Born on Wednesday

The situation is not easy, because your mind is concentrating on considerations that are irrelevant. Be constant, persevering, and firm. Then and only then will you have more self-confidence, and your chances of success will greatly improve.

Born on a Thursday

This is an excellent omen. Everything is favorable for you, and you will grow and develop. Continue along the same path, and you will achieve great success!

Born on a Friday

The answer to your question is "yes." You have many cards in your favor that will help you succeed, especially where love or artistic pursuits are concerned. Do not give in to sadness or lose motivation. Continue what you have started, and you will be successful.

Born on a Saturday

The answer to your question is "no" or "not yet." Your situation requires strength of character and even a reassessment of your objectives. When your mind is clearer you will be able to act, but not yet.

2 ⚬ Venus

Born on a Sunday

Be careful, this is a warning! If you have too much self-confidence, you will get nowhere. Nor will you succeed if you have too little confidence in yourself… This symbol asks you not to act immediately. Reconsider the situation, ask yourself the right questions, then come and consult the oracle a little later.

Born on a Monday

In this situation do not count on others to help you. Nor should you throw yourself into an ill-considered enterprise, because this would have unfortunate consequences. There are still efforts to be made, a task to be completed, and harmony to be created within a relationship. You will be successful if you see the situation as it really is and not as you would like it to be…

Born on a Tuesday

Yes, the omen is favorable, and you will complete your project successfully so long as you do not allow yourself to be influenced by what others are saying or thinking. Have a clear objective, solve the problems one after the other, without rushing, and rely only on yourself to complete this project successfully. Then you will definitely succeed.

Born on a Wednesday

No, for the time being you do not have sufficient determination and willpower to realize your plans. You still need some information or grounds for comparison. For the moment reconsider your position and see people as they really are without fooling yourself. It is through perseverance, self-confidence, and work well done that you will achieve your objective, but a little later.

Born on a Thursday

The omen is not entirely favorable for you. Obstacles remain, and there is not yet any harmony. In order to make progress, you must be receptive rather than active, flexible not rigid. Understand the motives of others; do not try to achieve everything all at once, and be patient. Learn how to distinguish between what is important and what is superfluous. Get rid of what weighs upon you and of the ideas that hold you back. Your frame of mind will change and you will consult the oracle again, at the proper time.

Born on a Friday

Yes, indeed! It is an excellent symbol that will help you achieve great success. Be determined and have confidence in yourself. Follow your intuition and remain true to yourself at all times. Your actions must be in agreement with your words. It is the key to a success that promises to be brilliant.

Born on Saturday

The situation is slightly to your advantage, but there are still a few things to clarify or organize. You must bring harmony into relationships and equilibrium into a situation. Do not give up, and do not lose your motivation. Do not be stopped by restrictive ideas but persevere, make an effort, with others or with one person in particular. Set yourself achievable goals and you will succeed.

3 ● Saturn

Born on a Sunday

Things are going your way, but you must still look for help or support. Consider the motivations of others, listen to what they have to say, understand their position, and you will understand your own better. Association is better than independence. Your task is not yet accomplished, and there are still some obstacles. Perseverance, loyalty to your commitments, and honesty in your feelings will help you to do the right thing to succeed a little later.

Born on a Monday

You are not in a favorable position. You lack clarity in your judgment, your plans are still rather vague, the task is not yet completed, and your relationship has not yet reached a satisfactory equilibrium. Do not remain fixated on the same problems or the same questions. See things from a distance, in a more detached, more serene manner. That way you will find new ways to succeed, a new way of acting that corresponds better to the requirements of the situation.

Born on a Tuesday

You feel torn between several options. The omen you have just drawn indicates that you have chances of succeeding as long as you don't act rashly or prematurely. For the moment, order your thoughts, decide on your priorities, but do not give up if your objective appears distant or if difficulties persist. Perseverance is needed. Consult the oracle again later.

Born on a Wednesday

The omen you have just drawn is good, if you are prepared to make efforts, and if you allow yourself to be influenced by the opinion of others or the general situation. Yes, of course, the battle is not entirely won, and some inertia or slowing down may still delay things. Be aware of what you want and act accordingly, following your deepest feelings. If you do so, you will have a good chance of success.

Born on a Thursday

No, frankly not, you are not in a position to succeed, or at any rate, not now. Your mind is confused, your project is vague and not mature enough, or you are deluding yourself. Ask yourself the real questions. Don't give in to impulsiveness, passion, or a passing fad. Consult the oracle again when the situation is clearer.

Born on a Friday

The situation is not easy and in theory you cannot influence others and bring your project to a successful conclusion. Nevertheless, in the medium term there are chances of success if you don't give in to impatience, and especially if you don't look for personal gain from this enterprise. You must have a broader vision; do not be in a hurry to reach your goal. Time is on your side.

Born on a Saturday

The omen you have just drawn promises great success. Indeed, the omen is excellent, if you rely not on chance but on your own abilities. It is your efforts, creativity, and sincerity towards yourself that lead you to success. Have confidence, persevere and… you will succeed.

4 ●The Sun

Born on a Sunday

Well done! You have just drawn an excellent omen. You will bring your enterprise to a successful conclusion. Don't be impatient, continue along the same path, and be sincere and steadfast. If you follow this guidance, your success will be complete.

Born on a Monday

You are in a frame of mind that promises success. You have a good chance of achieving your aims, as long as you do not become lazy or lose motivation. You still need to make the right decisions. Beware of overestimating your powers, but at the same time don't sell yourself short. Learn to appreciate and encourage yourself whenever the need arises. Make sure you have a clear view of the situation, and do not mistake your wishes for reality. Have a dialogue with yourself and follow your intuition, your inner voice. It will lead you to success.

Born on a Tuesday

The situation in which you find yourself is not to your advantage. You should start by asking yourself clear, precise, serious questions. You must be disciplined. Moderate your appetites, and direct your energy towards an achievable goal instead of wanting everything at the same time. Then and only then should you consult the oracle again.

Born on a Wednesday

If you know what you want, if your intuition tells you to act, then go for it, you have a good chance of succeeding. But if you are not sure, if your mind is still confused or you still feel anxious, do not act.

Born on a Thursday

You are in a favorable position. Even if there are still some obstacles, misunderstandings or hesitancy to overcome, you will be able to resolve the situation. Act firmly in accordance with what you think and say. If you are able to have an open, honest, sincere dialogue with yourself, you will succeed.

Born on a Friday

Your position is uncomfortable. The ground on which you are moving is unstable, changing, or dangerous if you are unable to identify the pitfalls. Don't rush into things and don't give in to impatience or passion. For the moment you must reflect and build up your character.

Born on a Saturday

You are certainly within your rights, and your ambition is commendable. Yet problems remain; you are still encountering obstacles on the way. You must put things into perspective, stand back, and reassess the situation. First ask yourself honestly if your goal is achievable in the immediate future, if what you want is really what you need. Consult the oracle again a little later on.

5 • The Moon

Born on a Sunday

You are in a good position, but the time has not come yet for you to act in a decisive way. For the time being, just let things take their course. Act gently, and slowly, be diplomatic and consistent, always going in the same direction. You will see things more clearly, you will feel more confident again, you will be better able to recognize opportunities to act, your objectives will become clearer, more precise. Then you will consult the oracle again.

Born on a Monday

The oracle that you have just drawn is excellent and promises much success. Continue in the same manner while remaining sincere, spontaneous, persevering, and honest towards yourself and therefore towards others. If you do so, you will bring your plans to a successful conclusion.

Born on a Tuesday

Your situation is beginning to improve; things are picking up momentum, but for the time being you still have to make some efforts. You must be generous, open-minded, and diplomatic. Do not be impatient or impulsive. Continue with perseverance and serenity. Then chance will smile upon you, perhaps even unexpectedly.

Born on a Wednesday

The present situation is not easy, far from it. Do not expect qualities in others that you do not have yourself, and do not look for immediate personal gain; it's not in the cards. Reconsider the situation in a more detached, serene manner and consult the oracle again later.

Born on a Thursday

Your situation is in balance, but this equilibrium is fragile. By listening to yourself better, by asking the guidance of more influential, experienced people, you will find the right approach. You have a good chance of success as long as you see the situation as it really is and do not idealize it.

Born on a Friday

This is a symbol of good omen. You will be able to bring your project to a successful conclusion if you follow the flow instead of trying to go against it. Recognize your own talents and work at improving them. It is these qualities and not circumstances that will enable you to achieve success very soon.

Born on a Saturday

No, frankly no. You are not in a position to evolve positively, and you are coming up against forces that are greater than you. For the time being, make no decisions and do not take any action. With time, situations will change and your chances of success will be much greater. Then you will consult the oracle again.

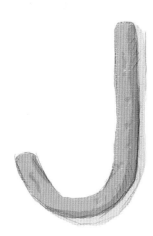

6 • Mars

Born on a Sunday

Your present situation does not allow you to express yourself freely, which prevents you from surmounting the obstacles in your way. Do not make any rash decision, and do not act ill-advisedly. You do not have all the necessary information and contacts at hand. You also lack a more global view of the situation. Redefine your goals and, if necessary, reappraise certain aspects of the problem. It is by separating the superfluous from the essential, by asking yourself the real questions, that you will discover the real answers.

Born on a Monday

The time is not right for large-scale, grandiose projects. Instead it calls for moderation. Your present situation is not unfavorable, but there are still some obstacles to be overcome. Make progress step by step, work on the details, and, if necessary, be flexible and patient if dependency on someone else is weighing you down. Continue to improve yourself and clarify your objectives. This will help you discover the means of achieving them.

Born on a Tuesday

The oracle that you have just drawn is excellent! You are very persuasive. You have self-confidence and are confident in your objectives. If you know exactly what you want and do not want, you will be able to overcome all your problems and to achieve success. Very soon.

Born on a Wednesday

You can create harmony in your relationships and achieve success in your enterprise as long as you do not convince yourself that you have arrived at the finish line... No, there are still problems to solve, work to be done, people to persuade, including yourself above all. You will succeed as long as you don't throw yourself rashly into a project but take the common good into account. On the other hand, selfish, petty-minded objectives are doomed to failure.

Born on a Thursday

Your present situation is not easy, being rather unstable and complex. Do not rebel against authority, do not lay the blame on anyone else but examine yourself more closely instead. For the moment, respect the natural order of things and know your place. Time is on your side as long as you give it a helping hand. Redefine your goals, draw up a stage-by-stage plan of action and approach these stages one after the other without any impatience. Only then should you consult the oracle again.

Born on Friday

If you are asking yourself questions, it is because there are questions to be asked… Examine your motivation, know what you want, and make sure that your goal is achievable. Then if it is not, reconsider your plans. You hold all the answers to your questions within yourself. By following your own intuition you will be able to comprehend them better and decide calmly. Consult the oracle again a little later.

Born on Saturday

Yes! The oracle is positive. The time has come to tackle the task ahead of you, to bring your actions and feelings under control so that they don't boil over. Your chances of success are great, but there are still efforts and adjustments to be made. Act with determination and deliberation, and you will succeed.

7 Mercury

Born on a Sunday

There are chances that your present situation will lead you to success as long as you do not pursue selfish objectives or demand immediate gratification.. Do not look for secret arrangements; your relationships must be clear, simple, and frank. Follow a noble objective, be generous, disinterested, and open to the opinion of others. Then you will triumph.

Born on a Monday

In the present situation you cannot act immediately because the oracle that you have just drawn indicates a lack of communication, some incomprehension or inertia. For the moment do not carry on with your projects. Prefer the shadow to the light. Do not be deluded by appearances, and do not delude yourself. Your qualities are real, but they are not yet recognized. Do not take action yet, and if necessary rethink certain aspects of your plans.

Born on a Tuesday

Your present situation is not easy. Your project is being hampered or your objectives have not been clearly defined. Nonetheless, there are chances of success in the medium term. But do not be in a rush to do well; wait a little while and try to find peace of mind, since this will enable you to take stock of the situation. Then, and only then, should you consult the oracle again.

Born on Wednesday

The oracle that you have just drawn is a very good omen. It promises success in your projects and recognizes that you are a gifted person. Continue along this path, do not have any doubts, and have confidence in yourself. It is your clear mind, your good judgment and your sincerity that will lead you down the road to success.

Born on a Thursday

Yes, the oracle favors you and is responding positively to your question. Yet there are still things to accomplish, relationships to improve and harmony to be found. You must have a strong will within you, but on the outside you must display sweetness and gentleness. Get rid of sad or discouraging thoughts, and learn how to share your happiness with other people. It is your enthusiasm that helps you triumph over obstacles.

Born on a Friday

The oracle you have just drawn says that violent or inconsiderate actions must be avoided. Indeed, you are not in a position of strength. Old problems, regrets or resentments cloud your judgment. Learn to put yourself in other people's shoes, understand their motives, and approach them without preconceived ideas. You must be patient, persevering, and consistent in your work, your ideas, and your relationships. Consult the oracle again a little later.

Born on a Saturday

Yes, you will achieve success, but before that there are efforts to be made. You must also clear your mind. Concentrate on rectifying the mistakes you may have made in the past, and do not allow the situation to deteriorate. Act calmly, follow your intuition, and remain honest with yourself. It is only when you have regained your self-confidence, when a weight has been taken off your chest, that you will be able to move towards success.

Kumalak

Shamanism from Kazakhstan

Since ancient times, along the Silk Road that crosses the steppes of Central Asia, the Shamans have been practicing Kumulak (which means "sheep dung") to predict the future. This art of divination almost disappeared in the seventeenth century under the upsurge of Islam, then during the Soviet regime, which banned its practice. Today Kumalak has made a comeback in Kazakhstan.

Consulting the oracle

1

Gather together forty-one small, easy to handle objects to use as tokens such as dried peas, broad beans, coffee beans, beads or pebbles… only metal is not allowed.

2

Sit down at a table and gather the forty-one tokens into a heap in front of you. Then separate these tokens into three heaps at random. Now take a piece of paper and draw a grid with nine numbered squares, as shown on the page opposite.

3

Now remove the tokens four at a time from the first heap, the one on the right. When there are only one, two, three or four tokens left, take them and put them in **square 1** of the grid. Put the other tokens you have just removed to one side for the moment.

4

Repeat the operation with the second heap, the one in the centre, and put one, two, three or four tokens in **square 2**.

5

Repeat the operation again with the third heap, the one on the left, and put the tokens in **square 3**.

6

Now take all the tokens you put to one side earlier on and gather them into one heap. Then divide this heap into three smaller heaps. Repeat the same operations described in stage 3, 4 and 5 in order to fill s**quares 4, 5, and 6**.

7

Finally, again take all the tokens put to one side and gather them into one heap. Then divide this heap into three smaller heaps. Repeat the same operations in order to fill **squares 7, 8, and 9.**

8

The remaining tokens will not be used.

9

Look at the grid. Add the tokens in squares 1, 2, and 3. The total should come to 5 or 9. Add the tokens in squares 4, 5, and 6. The result should be 4, 8 or 12 tokens. Add the tokens in squares 7, 8 and 9. Again, the result should be 4, 8, or 12 tokens.

If this is not the case you have made a mistake… start again!

Kumulak's grid interpreted line by line:

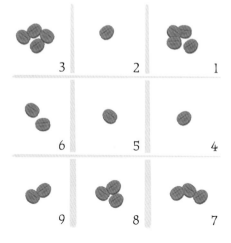

The **first line** (squares 1, 2, and 3) describes **the past and the state of mind** of the questioner.

The **second line** (squares 4, 5 and 6) describes **the present situation and the strengths and weaknesses** of the questioner.

The **third line** (squares 7, 8 and 9) refers to the future. It is the answer to the question, **the prediction for the future.**

Interpretations

First line: the state of mind

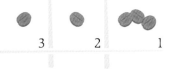

**"FIRE IN YOUR HEAD,
WIND IN YOUR EYES"**
Your thoughts are clear, generous, open to the world and to others around you. You believe in what you are doing and in the successful outcome of your plans. Your strengths are mobility, enthusiasm, and initiative.

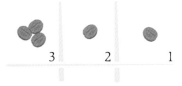

**"FIRE IN YOUR HEAD,
FIRE IN YOUR EYES"**
Your mind is turned towards what is positive, wide-ranging, and uplifting. Your self-confidence enables you to open doors, make situations develop, and motivate others. Do not fear either difficulties or competition.

**"FIRE IN YOUR HEAD,
WATER IN YOUR EYES"**
You feel the need to share. Love, affection, and tenderness are your main concerns. You are looking for happiness in your family life and a harmonious loving relationship. If your question is about children, your wishes will be granted.

**"FIRE IN YOUR HEAD,
SAND IN YOUR EYES"**
You seem concerned and disappointed. You are angry with someone or with yourself, or you are doubtful about the outcome of your project. Yet you know you are heading in the right direction.

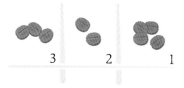

"WATER IN YOUR HEAD, WATER IN YOUR EYES"

Things are not evolving as you would like, or you are dependent on a person or situation. For the moment you do not hold the key to the problem.

"WATER IN YOUR HEAD, SAND IN YOUR EYES"

There is frustration, sadness, even anguish and suffering. You no longer know how to act, where to go or whom to appeal to.

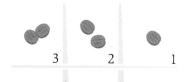

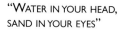

"WATER IN YOUR HEAD, FIRE IN YOUR EYES"

At first sight you seem full of good intentions, rather optimistic ones, but in reality your mind is not clear and your ideas are confused…

"WATER IN YOUR HEAD, WIND IN YOUR EYES"

On the outside you appear cheerful and content, but inside you are anxious, a problem keeps resurfacing, you are disappointed by someone or you are not sure of yourself.

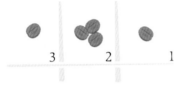

3   2   1

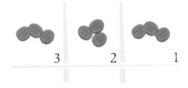

3   2   1

"WIND IN YOUR HEAD, FIRE IN YOUR EYES"

Motivated, enthusiastic, and optimistic … your ideas are clear and your objectives well defined. This positive attitude enables you to bring any project to a successful conclusion.

"THE THREE STARS"

These three stars protect you. There is no need to ask the Kumalak any more questions! Everything will be all right, even better than you might expect!

3   2   1

3   2   1

"WIND IN YOUR HEAD, SAND IN YOUR EYES"

You are frightened of doing wrong, of not measuring up. You have suffered and someone has hurt you. Although for the time being events do not seem to support your opinion, you know that you are following the right path.

"WIND IN YOUR HEAD, WATER IN YOUR EYES"

Obstacles are blocking your way. You know that you are following the right path, but the confusion of other people or of one person in particular hampers you.

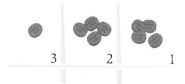

"SAND IN YOUR HEAD, SAND IN YOUR EYES"

You are plagued by anxiety, you are asking yourself endless questions, or an obstacle seems to be insurmountable. You feel weighed down by worries, and you have lost your points of reference. You are very dependent on others.

"SAND IN YOUR HEAD, WATER IN YOUR EYES"

Your ideas fail to elicit any response and other people are refusing to be influenced. You cannot see how to make your dreams come true, and this makes you feel gloomy.

"SAND IN YOUR HEAD, WIND IN YOUR EYES"

You have every reason to be happy but you are missing something or someone… You want to act, but the situation seems to be deadlocked, or an old problem is resurfacing.

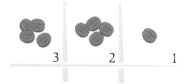

"SAND IN YOUR HEAD, FIRE IN YOUR EYES"

You appear to be strong and motivated, but you do not know what others are expecting from you. Behind a detached and confident appearance, you fear the future.

Second line: the current situation

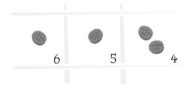

"FIRE IN YOUR HEART, WATER IN YOUR HANDS"

Your situation is encouraging, because your heart is pure, but you lack resources, weight or conviction. For the moment the balance of power is not in your favor.

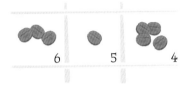

"FIRE IN YOUR HEART, EARTH IN YOUR HANDS"

You have the mental and emotional strength to improve your situation, to start and develop a relationship. Your intuition tells you that you are following the right path.

"FIRE IN YOUR HEART, FIRE IN YOUR HANDS"

You are not yet capable of initiating or taking charge of a project. A task has not yet been completed, or a relationship has not yet become stable.

"FIRE IN YOUR HEART, WIND IN YOUR HANDS"

You have a certain inferiority complex in relation to others and you lack self-confidence. But you have every chance of making up for these drawbacks.

"WATER IN YOUR HEART, FIRE IN YOUR HANDS"

The situation is not to your advantage. You heart is heavy, and if your state of mind does not change you will become increasingly confused. Yes, anxiety is a bad counselor.

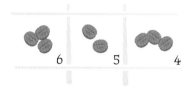

"WATER IN YOUR HEART, WIND IN YOUR HANDS"

You want to bring equilibrium into your relationships but you are feeling rather apprehensive. Your position is fragile because you are not sure of yourself. You must first learn to trust yourself more.

"WATER IN YOUR HEART, EARTH IN YOUR HANDS"

You do not really know how to behave, and others are in a similar position. You have strengths that for the moment cannot come to the fore.

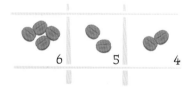

"WATER IN YOUR HEART, WATER IN YOUR HANDS"

You are full of doubts, you are feeling vulnerable, tormented, and worried, and this is reflected in your relationships. You cannot make any decision yet. Where health is concerned, you must be very careful.

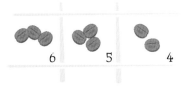

"WIND IN YOUR HEART, EARTH IN YOUR HANDS"

You are starting with a strong hand and great physical and mental strengths. Your heart is open to the world, and you feel ready for new experiences in your life.

"WIND IN YOUR HEART, WATER IN YOUR HANDS"

You have a feeling of inferiority. You depend on others or on a particular person. This situation, which is not to your advantage, could depress you, but it does not because you know that you are following the right path.

"WIND IN YOUR HEART, WIND IN YOUR HANDS"

You feel capable of surmounting the obstacles on your way but those who are facing you are less fortunate. The scales are tipping… in your favor.

"WIND IN YOUR HEART, FIRE IN YOUR HANDS"

Your dependence on others is almost total. You are not strong enough to make the situation develop in your favor. You can, however, remain calm and serene.

"SAND IN YOUR HEART, WIND IN YOUR HANDS"

Your heart is heavy with sadness. You are asking yourself all sorts of disordered questions, you are feeling held back, and you are submerged in your emotions. Your view of the situation is not the right one…

"SAND IN YOUR HEART, FIRE IN YOUR HANDS"

Your thoughts are confused, you are frightened or are experiencing doubts. For the time being you are not equipped to overcome the obstacles that are in your way.

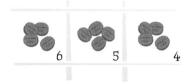

"SAND IN YOUR HEART, WATER IN YOUR HANDS"

A difficult situation and potential source of conflict. You seem lost and feel exhausted by the same questions that keep cropping up in the same way. You no longer know who to turn to.

"SAND IN YOUR HEART, EARTH IN YOUR HANDS"

Many ideas, many plans… you are aware of the strengths within you that are waiting to reveal themselves. So why this sadness?

Third line: prediction of the future

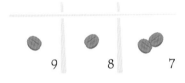

"WATER RIDER ON FIRE HORSE"

Prediction

You are guided by impulsiveness and passion, but you do not possess sufficient weight or stability to realize your intentions. You are temporarily blocked by circumstances.

Attitude to adopt

Curb your enthusiasm, wait for a better moment to act, and do not feel frustrated if the situation does not develop at the speed that you would like.

"FIRE RIDER ON FIRE HORSE"

Prediction.

There is action and mobility in this symbol. Embark upon new ventures. It is a favorable time for traveling, moving, transforming or starting a project. Maintaining the status quo is not recommended.

Attitude to adopt

Be thirsty for freedom and independence, do not stay at home or in the same place. Go out. You will find what you are looking for somewhere else, with others, or in an unexpected way.

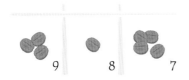

"EARTH RIDER ON FIRE HORSE"

Prediction

This is a very positive augury. The success of your enterprise lies in your own hands. Financial gains, success, renown, well-being. For a man this portends a serious relationship, marital happiness, or a wedding!

Attitude to adopt

Be open to new things. You don't have to go anywhere. Good news will come to you.

"WIND RIDER ON FIRE HORSE"

Prediction

Success lies in remaining mobile. There is a promise of beneficial change and satisfaction. A woman who draws this response can expect a serious relationship even marriage. If you are already married, it is sure to be a happy one.

Attitude to adopt

Make a decision or take actions now. By going to meet others, by making a move or traveling, you will find success.

"FIRE RIDER
ON WATER HORSE"

Prediction

This symbol is not a good omen. It speaks of difficulties, a disagreement, solitude or the need to retreat.

Attitude to adopt

You are going off course; you are mistaken. Reappraise the various aspects of your project that no longer reflect reality.

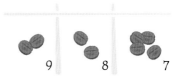

"EARTH RIDER
ON WATER HORSE"

Prediction

This symbol gives a positive answer to your question, but you must not be too impatient, act rashly or look for outside help.

Attitude to adopt

You are on the right track but not all problems have been solved. You must persevere, make the necessary efforts and do not count on anyone to help you.

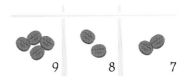

"WIND RIDER ON WATER HORSE"

Prediction
Tensions, problems with others or with someone in particular… There is going to be a power struggle, a conflict, a confrontation or a break-up.

Attitude to adopt
You are forced to change direction and tackle the situation in a different way. Do not wait before choosing a new course of action. Change your state of mind and be prepared to make a difficult decision.

"WATER RIDER ON WATER HORSE

Prediction
Your situation could improve provided that you are able to control your emotions. There are still internal tensions that need to be dealt with and problems within yourself that you must resolve.

Attitude to adopt
Behave in a more straightforward manner and be more open to new ideas. Then people will come towards you. Remember that in your situation the final decision is not up to you.

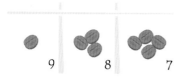

9   8   7

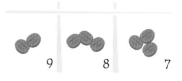

9   8   7

"EARTH RIDER
ON WIND HORSE"

Prediction

This is a very good omen! Don't worry, your situation will improve considerably!

Attitude to adopt

Have faith. Do not look elsewhere for answers. You possess all that's required to live better and more happily.

"WIND RIDER
ON WIND HORSE"

Prediction

This symbol speaks of movement and transformation. It indicates more a change in your state of mind than in material conditions.

Attitude to adopt

Speed up your pace, and do not be influenced by the lack of motivation in others. At the same time do not try to reach your goal at any cost. Your situation will improve as result of something unexpected.

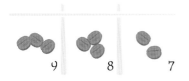

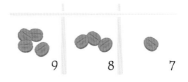

"WATER RIDER ON WIND HORSE"

Prediction

Your problems are in the process of being resolved, but things are still out of balance. You can't act freely. You want to go forward, but something or someone is standing in your way.

Attitude to adopt

The situation is improving, but you must not rush anything. The time to act has not yet come. Be patient.

"FIRE RIDER ON WIND HORSE"

Prediction

You must be prepared to travel. Success will come from an outside source, and someone will make your task easier.

Attitude to adopt

Act, communicate, travel. Exchange points of view. You are dealing with the right people.

9   8   7

9   8   7

"WIND RIDER
ON EARTH HORSE"

Prediction

This symbol promises the successful out-come of your projects, the stabilization of your position, and the fulfillment of your expectations.

Attitude to adopt

Continue along the same path without rushing anything. The situation will improve. Someone is bringing good news.

"WATER RIDER
ON EARTH HORSE

Prediction

This symbol speaks of isolation, slowing down, and a lack of freedom. Before you can influence the course of events, you must wait for tensions to disappear or for a calmer state of mind.

Attitude to adopt

You are dependent on others or over-taken by events. You cannot make any progress, and no one can get near you. Do not act rashly: this blockage is only temporary; soon these restricting cir-cumstances will disappear

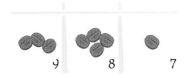

9   8   7   9   8   7

"FIRE RIDER
ON EARTH HORSE"

"MOTHER EARTH"

Prediction
This symbol speaks of riches and well-being. Your situation will soon improve noticeably. Success is here, close to you or in your home.

Attitude to adopt
There are no great projects to undertake and no traveling. All you have to do is to remain available. A person whom you like will contact you bearing good news.

Prediction
This is the best symbol in the Kumalak! It promises good fortune, success, good health, and travel. It speaks of wisdom, shared love, and material acquisitions. You will achieve your goal!

Photo Credits: